I0027986

Transitions

Adjustment Strategies of American Immigrants

Marvin H. Shaub

University Press of America,® Inc.
Lanham · Boulder · New York · Toronto · Plymouth, UK

Copyright © 2009 by
University Press of America,® Inc.
4501 Forbes Boulevard
Suite 200
Lanham, Maryland 20706
UPA Acquisitions Department (301) 459-3366

Estover Road
Plymouth PL6 7PY
United Kingdom

All rights reserved
Printed in the United States of America
British Library Cataloging in Publication Information Available

Library of Congress Control Number: 2009927841
ISBN-13: 978-0-7618-4679-6 (paperback : alk. paper)
ISBN-10: 0-7618-4679-4 (paperback : alk. paper)
eISBN-13: 978-0-7618-4680-2
eISBN-10: 0-7618-4680-8

⊖™The paper used in this publication meets the minimum
requirements of American National Standard for Information
Sciences—Permanence of Paper for Printed Library Materials,
ANSI Z39.48-1992

To Bill Lombardo—

A Great Man, A Great Friend

Contents

Preface

Who are you?

This question seems simple enough. Most people would answer with their name. I am John Smith. I am Mary Brown.

But suppose you are the former Mary Brown who is now married to Phillip Jones. Who are you now? Are you still Mary Brown? Are you Mary Jones? Have you changed in any way from having been married to Phillip Jones? If you are headed to your high school reunion the answer might be different from what it usually is, as many of the people you will see there might still think of you as Mary Brown. Could you be Mary Brown-Jones? Are you having lunch with other women who believe in maintaining a dual identity, bridging past and present? Under what circumstances could you be Mrs. Phillip Jones?

Suppose you are a member of a championship sporting team and the coach, eager to bump up morale, shouts the question at you—are you then a New York Giant or a Pittsburgh Penguin, sacrificing your individual separateness for the sake of team spirit? You are religiously devout and your clergyman asks who you are—are you then a devoted but individually nameless Servant of God? If you are at the social security office you could answer that you are number 123-456-7890 if that happens to be your social security number. If you are a Hispanic woman and your formal name is Gabriela Garcia de Cardenas a person not familiar with Latino naming convention could think you are Gabriela Cardenas, Gabriela de Cardenas or Gabriela Garcia. Even at the simple level of conveying to someone else how he or she should refer to you context comes into play, as well as your own personal preferences and ways you have chosen to adjust to changing circumstances.

Who are you? This book is about how immigrants to America have come to ponder the deeper meaning of this question and what the answers have been for many of them—at least at particular times. In looking back and then considering the present I will discuss changes in American demography, sociological development, technology and individual adjustment factors which have come into play to affect the choices American immigrants have had and the choices they have made. The book is about identity—that sense of self that makes each person unique, the combination of ways each of us appropriates bits and pieces from our nationality, our ethnicity, our race, our religion, our family, our friends, the media we are exposed to and many other sources of experiences that no other person can claim to have—what we have brought with us from the past combined with social relationships and perceptions of society, institutions and other "realities" we are experiencing now.

Suppose you suddenly feel hungry and would like a bite to eat. If you are at a sporting event and the only food available comes from the hotdog stand then your choices are to remain hungry or to eat the hotdog. If you at a coffee shop chances are you can still have the hotdog but alternatively you might choose one of the other meals on the menu. Maybe you have chosen a little fancier type of restaurant enabling you to construct a meal from more widely differing pieces—perhaps your original hotdog but now supplemented by a piece of gourmet sushi. Perhaps you would like some Tiramisu for dessert and maybe a glass of wine imported from some faraway place. You now have many choices and can adjust to being hungry in a larger number of ways.

For about the first two hundred years of its modern cultural existence America was in a sense like the hotdog stand. Most of the immigrants, at least those we read the most about, tended to be from England or other places in Northern Europe. Most came from similar cultural backgrounds, lifestyles and ways of relating to each other. The denizens of this more or less *Uni-cultural America* came often in search of improved economic opportunity, and in some cases more religious freedom. There were other cultures present, such as Native Americans and later individuals we now know as African Americans. But the three cultures tended to develop separately, whether by choice or not, each keeping more or less to itself—as opposed to mixing or blending in with the then dominant culture.

Late in the nineteenth century many different types of immigrants began arriving in America. As before they were European but a different type of European—often coming from Eastern or Southern Europe, speaking languages unfamiliar to those already here, with urban rather than rural lifestyles and often professing Catholic or Jewish faith rather than the Protestantism of the earlier immigrants. These so called "new" immigrants were often not simply seeking more freedom or more money. They were often fleeing for their lives, or away from serious and unfortunate consequences that would have likely befallen them had they stayed in Europe. They were here seeking a new start—they were "the huddled masses yearning to breathe free" of Lazarus' famous poem now enshrined at the base of The Statue of Liberty. But, in fact, they were often not welcome by the "old" immigrants, who wanted America to stay as it was. Thus was born our first large-scale encounter with *acculturational stress*—the need to deal with prolonged contact with people from cultures very different from one's own.

Like moving from the hotdog stand to the sandwich shop these new immigrants did have some choice in how they adjusted. They could blend in to what came to be known as The Great American Melting Pot ("No matter my background I am proud to be an American"). They could stay apart and form societies of their own ("I like it here in Little Italy. Many that live here have not forgotten the old ways"). They could have some of each ("I am proud to be Russian-American. I mix tomato juice with my vodka"). Or they could adjust in other ways.

Many scholarly debates arose about immigrant adjustment to America and just where we were headed. These sometimes spilled over into everyday discourse and even entertainment. Will America develop as a group of separate cultural states, maybe with different languages as in Canada? Or will it mix people of different backgrounds together to make a whole that is somehow greater than the sum of its parts? Questions like these will be addressed in the early chapters of this book.

About two thirds of the way through the twentieth century some changes in immigration law led to very substantial changes in both the numbers of immigrants coming to America and their origin points. Immigration was no longer mostly about Europe. Increasingly it came to be about Latin America and The Far East. American demography began to change as well. So too did the type of society we have. A mode of adjustment often referred to as *Bi-Culturality* began to emerge within this growing pool of newcomers—the idea being that immigrants from non-European origin points tended to want to keep their previous identities while building separate American identities—each to be available as circumstances required. Some Bi-Culturals chose to eat both the hotdog and the sushi.

A new and energetic cohort of social scientists came into prominence, often emanating from the Latin or Far Eastern cultures they were studying and writing about. New questions began to be debated—is it really possible for the same person to develop two different personalities? How is the broader pre-existing society affected by the ways of the newcomers? Chapter Two will provide a brief literature review to highlight some of the thinking that developed during that time. I will discuss the work of Professor John Berry, a cross-cultural psychologist from Canada who developed a model of individual adjustment that I consider useful in understanding some of these issues—a model which takes two axes of development into account: one from the previous culture and one from the new culture and also develops corresponding axes for environmental settings presented by receiving societies thereby tieing together psychological (individual) and sociological (group) influences. I will present a refinement for part of the Berry model which I developed myself to place a person more precisely in bi-cultural space, the degree to which they have become *fully bicultural* and thus able to act and react in each culture as someone who is *unicultural* in that culture. This model, based on my own experiences in life and in international business, is called *ACES*—an acronym for Anchoring, Communication, Enjoyment and Sensitivity.

More recently a model of adjustment referred to as *Hybrid Culturality* has come to be a popular topic. This is a form of adjustment where a strong basic core personality is added onto by appropriation of pieces corresponding to the particular experiences an individual has had. Some refer to this type of personality as a *pastiche*. In Chapter Five I use the segment of immigrant Muslims as an illustration of how many, but of course not all, develop in this way.

At this point in the book I will have covered a range of orientations open to immigrants to America as the country progressed and developed—from the limited options of the Unicultural America of primarily Northern Europeans to the increasing array of options presented to the "new" immigrants from other parts of Europe to the Bi-Cultural possibilities enabled by the more recent prominence of those from Latin America and The Far East to the even broader array of possibilities inherent in the Hybrid Culture construction. The hotdog stand had turned into the coffee shop, which in turn became a restaurant and finally a huge cafeteria of cultural choices.

Next we come to the America of the mid-1990s, an America which was to witness a revolution so profound that the very ideas of the hotdog stand, the coffee shop, the restaurant and the cafeteria had to be rethought. This was the revolution in information technology.

In a short period of time we have come to experience an explosion of technology, a world of previously undreamed of expansion in connectivity, in instant access to a huge variety of information, in time-space compression and in the availability—not just within the borders of America but worldwide—of a different kind of existential experience. I call this *The Ether-World*: a world entered and exited at will via the connection with information technologies and representing an endogenous counterpart, a condition that comprises relationship with both technology and potentially with other people articulated in an electronic cosmos. The Ether-World has allowed those who are inclined to depart farther and farther away from the ties that have bound them to a particular culture. It has enabled, for some, an era of *Post-Culturality*. Potential immigrants no longer need to wait to arrive in America to experience American life realistically and in detail. Those who have already arrived here can simultaneously enlarge their relationship with America and its (usually) different society while maintaining contact with their traditional society, family, old friends and others.

This will be the story of the development of acculturation in America as a distinct social process. The conditions I have described briefly in this Preface, and which I will develop in more detail in the balance of the book, are not sequential for an individual—ie. one does not necessarily progress from one to the next as in many concepts of personality development. Indeed one can enter and exit these modes of adjustment as individual circumstances and needs for adjustment change. That is why it is so fascinating for me. And why I hope it will be for you as well.

Marvin H. Shaub, Ph.D.   November 2008
Princeton, New Jersey
USA

Acknowledgments

This book began in 2005 as a doctoral dissertation. Looking back on those busy days I would like to thank Professor Kenneth J. Gergen of Swarthmore College, my main dissertation advisor, who always knew the right questions to ask and when to ask them. His support and insight throughout the writing process were of great value to me as was his excellent text editing. My Ph.D. was awarded by Tilburg University in Tilburg, The Netherlands. In that regard I would like to thank my Dutch advisor Professor John B. Rijsman for his valuable assistance in coordinating my efforts with those of the University.

I would like to thank Professor Filipe Korzenny of Florida State University, Mr. Steven Palacios of Cheskin Research and Ms. Isabel Valdes for providing initial versions of some of the ideas found in my text, particularly with respect to Hispanics. Professor Korzenny was also helpful in providing key initial reading suggestions. My good friend Sr. Roberto Torres of Reseda, California provided substantial input that allowed me to understand more clearly some complicated relationships Hispanics have with each other and with mainstream American society.

I thank many of the people of The Islamic Society of Central Jersey, particularly Imam Hamam Chebli and Mr. Moustafa Zayyed, for reaching out to me and helping me understand some of the more intricate parts of the Muslim culture. Additionally I thank our many Japanese and other Asian friends for helping me develop the Far Eastern aspects of the book. I particularly appreciate the formative contributions, some time ago, of Dr. Yukio Ishizuka. Additionally, I wish to thank the many individuals who gave generously of their time in order to provide input for the narrative sections of the book. My thanks go out to The Princeton University Library System, librarians and staff for the many courtesies and helpful support they have extended to me. I acknowledge and thank Mr. Veezhinathan Jayaraman for his expert help in the portions of the manuscript that required computer graphics and other computer technology. I express my appreciation to the expert staff of my publisher University Press of America, particularly Brooke Bascietto and Brian DeRocco. And I express particular gratitude to Dorothy Albritton of Majestic Wordsmith, without whose help in formatting, editing and other aspects of manuscript preparation this book would probably never have been finished.

I would like to thank the members of my family—my wife Yuko, daughters Lisa and Nicole and sons Eric and Joshua, plus the spouses and children of those who are adults—for their support in my earlier doctoral endeavor and in the writing of this book. Finally I express my appreciation to my late mother Edith Shaub for her encouragement in my early years of explorations in serious writing. To all the above listed, and to the many others who supported me in so many ways, I express my sincere gratitude.

Chapter ONE

Orientations to Immigration and Acculturation

In the mists of pre-history natural migrations of early men and women may eventually have resulted in contact between groups that had previously-developed dissimilar cultures. In those far distant times, as in more modern ones, such contact—if carried on over a long period—would likely have required some combination of adjustments to be made if even relative harmony was to prevail over chaos. These adjustments to stresses brought on by prolonged exposure to unusual or different cultures came to be known as *acculturation*.

On the scholarly level the term *acculturation* has come to include many different things—anthropological constructs, psychological constructs, sociological constructs among them. Researchers have taken acculturation to be mainly concerned with domains of cognition, values, behaviours, knowledge, beliefs, self-concepts, ethnic identities or combinations of these. I will utilize many of these frameworks to analyze acculturation from the viewpoint of its development as a complex social process among immigrants to America.

The balance of this initial chapter will be primarily devoted to establishing perspective through discussion of migration activity—dealing first with the global picture then homing in more closely on immigration phenomena in America. A final section will provide a transition to the study of American immigrant acculturation.

The Magnitude of the Migration Issue in the World

The amount of migration that is going on around the world has increased sharply in recent years. The United Nations (2006, p. 1) estimated that, in the year 2005, there were 190.6 million migrants in the world, up from 165.1 million in 1995 (an increase of 15.4%) and up from 111.0 million in 1985 (an increase of 71.7%). Currently 3% of the world's population comprises migrants—people now living in a different country from that in which they were born (United Nations, ibid, p. 1). In some areas however the figure is much higher. For example, The International Organization for Migration estimates that, currently, 7.7% of Europe's population comprises migrants. The comparable figure for North America is 12.9% (International Organization for Migration, 2005, p. 255). If all the world's migrants were grouped together as one country they would comprise the world's fifth largest nation. Clearly, this is a substantial aggregate of people.

Of particular concern is the sub-population of unauthorized migrants, for whom acculturation presents additional obstacles. It is estimated that there are some 30 to 40 million unauthorized migrants on the world scene. The US is estimated to have about 12 million of these (Passel, 2006, pp. i and ii), whereas Europe has an estimated 8 million (International Organization for Migration, op. cit, p. 255). Often these unauthorized, undocumented people face the bleakest of futures once their original migratory causation has run its course (for example, outsourcing and exportation of factory jobs that represented the original attraction).

While not always true, generally speaking migrants tend to move to countries that are technologically more advanced than the countries they came from. The International Organization for Migration lists the three countries receiving the most immigrants, as of the year 2000, as The United States, Russian Federation and Germany. The next two were Ukraine and France. So it is often true that immigrants enter a world of contextual surprises, where previously unknown machinery of life and ways of doing things await to stretch and shape them. They are challenged to adjust to differences in their self-understanding, their beliefs, values and ways of life.

The issue of understanding and dealing responsibly with immigrants (as well as minority or subservient cultures already in place) and making their acculturation (or other types of adjustment) easier has become a significant international issue. For example, adjustment problems of Muslims who originally came to Europe seeking work have resulted in riots, bombings and significant loss of life. Recent genocide episodes in Africa and Eastern Europe have revived memories of the Holocaust. Further, as this document is being written there are significant movements going on in many parts of the world (including The United States) to prevent, reduce or discourage immigration and to enforce rigid and often unrealistic rules on those already at their new destinations. For example, the French ruling that Muslim girls could not wear headscarves in school was viewed by the dominant culture as a means of securing inclusivity, whereas for the Muslim culture it was interpreted as discriminatory.

Immigration in America

It has been said that America is a country of immigrants. This is true, in the sense that life did not originate here. Many scholars subscribe to the theory that 15,000 years or so ago hunters from what is now Siberia crossed over the Land Bridge now submerged beneath the Bering Strait and, when it became feasible, moved southward to become the "indigenous peoples"—free standing cultures—inhabiting North, Central and South America (see Footnote 1.1). The peoples who settled in what later developed into The United States of America became known as Native Americans.

Permanent settlements by Europeans began with Jamestown, Virginia in 1607. Gradually more settlers from England and other parts of Northern Europe emigrated to America. By 1790 about 75% of the 3.9 million people living in territory now included in the United States were from either England or Germany (see Footnote 1.2). Of the balance, about 75% were African individuals brought here during the period beginning around 1640 (and culminating in 1865) to serve as slaves.

An early historical look at modern day US immigration is provided by de Tocqueville in his classic *Democracy in America*, written in 1835. A French civil servant from an aristocratic background, he often referred to the American people of the time as "Anglo-Americans"—inferring a body of more or less homogeneous English immigrants. De Tocqueville described a young, uni-cultural America—rich in promise, potential and resources there for the taking. He said (p. 177):

It would be difficult to describe the avidity with which the American rushes forward to secure this immense booty that fortune offers. In the pursuit he fearlessly braves the arrow of the Indian and the diseases of the forest; he is unimpressed by the silence of the woods, the approach of beast of prey does not disturb him, for he is goaded onwards by a passion stronger than the love of life.

De Tocqueville was impressed with the general equality he found in America—so different from the highly articulated class structures of many countries in Europe. He remarked (p. 3):

The more I advanced in the study of American society, the more I perceived that this equality of condition is the fundamental fact from which all others seem to be derived and the central point at which all my observations constantly terminated.

In constructing an America featuring equality of condition, however, de Tocqueville was referring only to the segment comprising Whites. He dismissed the two major minorities of the times, as mentioned briefly above—Negroes (as African Americans were then called) and Native American Indians. Negroes were brought to America from Africa, to work the plantations in the South by those de Tocqueville understood as like European aristocrats. The Negroes so involved lived a culturally marginalized life. He wrote:

The Negro of the United States has lost even the remembrance of (his) country; the language which his forefathers spoke is never heard around him; he abjured their religion and forgot their customs when he ceased to belong to Africa. But he remains half-way between the two communities, isolated between two races . . . (p. 201)

The only society that pre-dated the advent of the British settlers was the American Indian (The Native American). These de Tocqueville characterized as inferior in technology to the Europeans, who made no great attempt to integrate them but rather pushed them back as the European settlers advanced. He characterized the Indians this way:

It is impossible to conceive the frightful sufferings that attend these forced migrations. They are undertaken by a people already exhausted and reduced; and the countries to which the new-comers betake themselves are inhabited by other tribes, which receive them with jealous hostility. (p. 207)

Turning now to more modern times, for many years immigration flows to America conformed to The Immigration and Nationality Act of 1952 which updated country-specific immigration quotas initially established in 1924, essentially keeping the country of origin profile of The United States about the same as it historically had been. In an article in *The Wall Street Journal,* (Crossen, 2006) Cynthia Crossen describes the beginnings of this system as follows:

Under the so-called national origins system, created first on an 'emergency' basis in 1921 and renewed in a more restrictive form in 1924, the US census would count the number of foreign-born immigrants already in the U.S. and determine how many came from each country. Thereafter, 2% of the total of each nationality would be admitted annually. (The 1924 law fixed no quotas for immigrants from New World countries, including Canada and Mexico, whose seasonal laborers were crucial to the nation's farmers.)

To compute the number of people of each nationality living in the U.S. however, Congress used a little sleight of hand. Instead of utilizing the 1920, 1910 or 1900 censuses, it reached all the way back to the 1890 census to create its quota baselines.

Why turn the clock back more than 30 years to establish (then) current policy? Because before 1890, most immigrants came from northern and western Europe, including Britain . . . Germany, and other countries. Between 1890 and 1920, many more immigrants sailed from southern and eastern European countries . . . (p. B-1)

The US Office of Immigration Statistics (See Footnote 1.1) indicates that the main country of origin components of the population of The United States in 1790 were England/UK 2.5 million and Germany .3 million. English immigration continued heavy in the period 1851-1880 (6.7 million) but then dropped off to 1.6 million between 1881 and 1910 and declined further to .7 million between 1911 and 1930. Germany showed a similar pattern. However Italy, Greece and Russia, not even on the US radar screen in 1790, contributed .1 million immigrants in 1851-1880, then 5.3 million between 1881 and 1910 and 2.8 million between 1911 and 1930.

In 1965, the 1952 Immigration Act was amended to eliminate country quotas and allow those already here (including very large numbers of Hispanic migrant workers) to bring over other family members (See Footnote 1.3). According to the US Census Bureau, in the year 1960 75.0% of the foreign born population then living in The United States came from Europe, 9.4% from Latin America and 5.1% from Asia (all other = 10.5%). (US Bureau of the Census, 1999, Table 2). By the year 2000 only 15.8% were from Europe, 51.7% from Latin America and 26.4% from Asia (all other = 6.1%). In that same period the total number of foreign born increased from 9.7 million to 31.1 million. Of the 31.1 million foreign born living in The United States in 2000 21.6 million had come since 1980. Of these, 12.0 million came from Latin America and 6.1 million from Asia. Only 2.3 million came from Europe. (US Bureau of the Census, 2000, Summary File 4, QT, p. 14). Just as the weather condition of "snow" is constructed and understood as different from "rain" or "sunshine"—requiring a different agenda, at least for outside activity—the change in the aggregate corpus of immigrants required new social scientific thinking. This change is covered in Chapter TWO.

As some subsequent sections of this document will focus on Hispanics as an important minority sub-culture in America, it is important to take a look at their figures. On 17 October 2006 the population of the United States reached 300 million (US Bureau of the Census, 2006, website home page). According to The Pew Hispanic Center (the most up to date source of statistics about America's Hispanics) at the end of 2004 there were 40.4 million documented Hispanics in the country (Pew, 2005, p. 2). Additionally an estimated 78% of the estimated 12 million undocumented individuals in the US are believed to be Hispanic (Passel, 2006, pp. i and ii). This yields a total of 49.8 million total Hispanics, or about 17% of the US population currently. Hispanics have overtaken African-Americans as America's largest minority group. The US Census Bureau estimates that by the year 2050 nearly one person in four living in America will be of Hispanic origin (US Bureau of the Census, 2004 A, p. 1). This sheer size, along with the vibrancy of the culture, has—in my opinion—created a kind of "critical mass" situation in America, a situation that demands careful attention.

To quote a Pew Hispanic Center research report (Passel & Suro, 2005, p. 1):

As it continues to grow, the composition of the Hispanic population is undergoing a fundamental change: Births in the United States are out-pacing immigration as the key source of growth. Over the next twenty years this will produce an important shift in the makeup of the His-panic population with second generation Latinos—the US-born chil-dren of immigrants—emerging as the largest component of that population.

The Wall Street Journal reported that the US Hispanic population increased 1.3 million from 2004 to 2005. Of this amount, only 38.5% came from immigration. The balance came from Hispanics already liv-ing here. Comparable figures for Non-Hispanic Whites were 500,000 total population growth, 40% from immigration (Kronholz, 2006, p. A6).

The other major recent immigrant group came from The Far East. In 2003 there were 13.5 million people counted by the Census Bureau as Asian, up 12.5% from the year 2000 (US Bureau of the Census, 2004, p. 1) While in total this is a substantial group it is largely made up of sub-groups who come from somewhat different Asian cultures and speak different indigenous languages. In a special report for the US Census Bureau, Reeves & Bennet (2004, p. 1) reported the populations of major Asian sub-groups as follows: Chinese 2.4 million, Filipino 1.9 million, Asian Indian 1.6 million, Korean 1.1 million, Vietnamese 1.1 million, Japanese .8 million, all other Asian (no single group more than 200,000) 4.7 million.

The Stranger in Our Midst

Among the many things that happened in the early days of the twenty-first century were two rather surprising events that forced open the eyes of many Americans. I refer first to the availability of results from the 2000 Census of the United States, which by law enumerates the Ameri-can population every 10 years. The pages of the 2000 Census spoke with imputed authority through the stark language of numbers of a strange and, for some, threatening "person" who had entered the familiar, cozy room. This person didn't speak or act as Americans are supposed to. He didn't hear the same voices "we" hear. Rather the voices he heard spoke to him in Spanish or Chinese or some other seemingly exotic tongue. This new person represented the deepening river of immigrants now coming from Latin America and The Far East. The "we" in whose voice

I have been speaking was the generation upon generation of traditional Americans whose roots lay in Europe.

What was this new person like? How could we get to know him? What relationship would we have with him? These were important questions in the early twenty-first century. They were also difficult ones to answer. For like Janus, the ancient Roman God of entrances and exits, our new person had two faces—one pointing in each direction. The face we could see was the shining immigrant face similar to that which many of us remember from the now sepia-toned photographs of our parents and grandparents as they emerged from Ellis Island. The other face, pointing the other way and hidden from us, betrayed the longing for a deep-rooted culture left behind—a culture with a powerful and lingering allure, even if packaged in fading memories of the difficult day-to-day "real life" circumstances of the past.

The 2000 Census vividly documented something that had been going on for years, continuously building upon itself but below the cognitive radar screen of most of mainstream America. To see it presented now as a "big change" by an authoritative national organization with substantial credibility seemed for many a formidable challenge. Perhaps we should have been more observant of the changes. After all, America had prior experience with large numbers of immigrants from Africa who came onto the American scene with not only a different history and belief structure but a distinctively different and indelible appearance as well. The discord of The American Civil Rights movement showed all too clearly, at least in retrospect, the dangers that can come from ignoring— some would say subjugating—a substantial minority. Today our laws are different and many feel our culture has been enriched by what Black voices and Black talents bring to our society.

The second event to which I refer is the tragedy of September 11, 2001. For the first time since Pearl Harbor America had suffered a large magnitude attack at home. This time, however, the attack came not from a country that had form, boundaries or substance but from an amorphous trans-national religious movement—built around an ideology to which its protagonists were deeply committed. As history would reveal, America did not reside alone in the bull's eye. Subsequent terrorist attacks in London, Madrid, Israel, Egypt, Jordan, Saudi-Arabia, Bali, Indonesia and Mumbai, India along with the Paris riots, the assassination of Dutch film-maker Theo Van Gogh and the self-instituted exile of Ayaan Hirsi Ali showed us that the world had changed in significant ways.

Many felt that the days were gone when countries could disregard the presence and needs of minorities in their midst—minorities struggling to cope with local contemporary issues not even recognized by the mainstream while listening in the dark, late at night to voices whispering to them from afar of a different agenda. Gone were the days when governments could presume that the mainstream culture would automatically appeal to everyone within the borders of the country. What would now be required to build loyalty, to make immigrants feel welcome and to identify with the country they were in rather than with ideologies from outside? Gone were the days when any country—even if guarded, as America was, by oceans on its flanks—could afford to disregard ideas that began and thrived elsewhere. Gone were the days of presuming that immigrants were powerless, could do no harm and could be left to fend for themselves.

Certainly most in America and elsewhere felt that the days of safety were at an end. Random violence could now touch anyone. Here were the days when any immigrant could, beneath the surface, harbor ideas and potential for action quite different from what was outwardly portrayed. Here entered the days of distrust. But here as well were the days of opportunity. For if America could overcome its tendency to focus on deficit rather than opportunity (Barrett and Fry, p. 31) and open ourselves to non-American ways of life and adopt a relational rather than an absolutist posture, then a new era of global collaboration might begin. We stand now at the cross-roads.

Positioning Acculturation Study

Acculturation is only one of many types of adjustment to which immigrant communities are challenged throughout the world. Additionally the process not only affects first generation immigrants but often has a lingering generational effect—in some cases of indefinite duration. However, for analytical purposes, I will focus on acculturation alone and mainly as it pertains to immigrants.

Even though formal acculturation study began about 70 years ago the vast preponderance has been generated in the last 25 years, much of it in The United States. A substantial impetus was given to the field by a new generation of scholars from non-traditional American immigrant ethnicities, mainly Hispanic and Asian, who were largely writing about their own cultures as these have developed in America. Indeed the very nature of acculturation study has been heavily influenced by changes in American immigration patterns—based on changes in American immigration law and the re-defining of the agenda of ideas that were believed important.

The next chapter will contain a review of scholarly research work in this field. As a segue I will discuss the vision of *The Great American Melting Pot*, showing how it developed in America and what changes caused it to cede some of its traction to an alternative construct—*The Bi-Cultural Personality*.

Chapter TWO

The Rise and Decline of The Great American Melting Pot

A s we saw in Chapter ONE, the period of the late nineteenth and early twentieth centuries was marked by substantial increases in immigration to America, compounded by several factors. These "new" immigrants came from European cultures that were substantially different from those of the British, German and other Northern European peoples who came before. The new immigrants tended to be Catholic (and in some cases Jewish) rather than Protestant, often spoke languages unfamiliar to those already settled in America and often reflected urban rather than rural mindsets, lifestyles and ways of relating to others. These "new" immigrants were often fleeing adverse situations such as war, severe religious or ethnic persecution or food shortages. Starting over in America was a critical objective for many.

These "new" immigrants were often not welcomed by the "old" immigrants, who wanted to keep America the conservative, rural, Protestant society it had been. An example of the result was the 1924 quota law, previously described, intended to contain the new elements. Often there was severe discrimination against those newcomers who had made it to America. The conflict also led to debate among scholars of the time as to whether America in the future would more likely resemble a *homogenized* mixture of immigrants from diverse original backgrounds or a *plural society* where each distinct cultural group would essentially maintain its own individual identity. This debate, framed before the beginning of formal study of acculturation, was brought into public focus by a play entitled *The Melting Pot*. Written by Israel Zangwill, a talented writer of

British and Russian descent and capturing the essence of the debate, the play attracted large audiences and stimulated considerable discussion in the early twentieth century.

The Melting Pot

The play pointedly articulated one of the great social issues of the time. Representing a strongly assimilationist viewpoint it presented the character David, a violinist of Russian peasant heritage who, after growing up yearning for the freedom he imagined would be his if he could only get to America and finally succeeding in his quest for emigration, coined the phrase that would come to capture the feeling that the strength through the diversity permitted by America would comprise a more important formative value than traditional cultural maintainance. As further proof of the power of The Great American Melting Pot, David successfully courts the play's character Vera—a former Cossack woman who would have been considered on the other side of class and ethnic divides in Russia and therefore out of his reach. Thernstrom (2004) provides this perspective:

> Zangwill's drama was a hymn to the power of assimilative forces in American life. The hero and heroine—he a Russian Jew, she a Cossack—could never have fallen in love and married in the Old World, but in America their historically antagonistic backgrounds were irrelevant. (p. 48)

The idea that America was a kind of crucible in which all types of immigrants could be molded into somewhat loosely defined polyglot Americans became popular as a rationale for that particular avenue of adjustment. Millions of immigrants, driven by dissociation from their former lives in Europe, gladly considered taking their place in The Great American Melting Pot. Indeed the main social impact of the play was to give voice and lend credence to a viewpoint that was welcomed by many of the more recent newcomers.

However not all European immigrants of the time felt that way. Many from wide ranges of backgrounds considered carefully whether they wished to subscribe to a new homogeneous mono-culture—with roots often far different from their own but nevertheless often consistent with their reasons for emigrating, including the experience of living in a more open society.

Some immigrants chose alternatives to The Melting Pot. Many, facing an often negative welcome in America by preceding cohorts, pursued a serious intent to separate and start completely new individual lives in America based on kinship felt with others of their original ethnicity. Many cities in America today maintain distinct sections dominated not by mainstream American culture but by particular ethnicities (e.g., Little Italys, Polish Sections, Chinatowns) that have descended from that era. Other immigrant groups of the time pursued a hyphenated ethnicity (e.g., Polish-American, Italian-American) that, in my view, for each pairing articulated a dual identity with separate original and new components that mixed together into a brew that did not correspond completely with either one identity or the other. This type of unitary but blended identity still characterizes the outlook of many Americans who are not quite ready to leave the ethnicities they grew up with completely behind or submerged.

In relatively recent times some scholars have put forward the idea that America today still conforms to the assimilative Melting Pot model. Here are the words of Barone, written in 2001:

> What is important now is to discard the notion that we are at a totally new place in American history, that we are about to change from a white-bread nation to a collection of peoples of color. On the contrary, the new Americans of today, like the new Americans of the past, can be interwoven into the fabric of American life. (p. 279)

While some would agree with this idea, I believe the appropriate way to conceptualize The Melting Pot period was that it was at one time a valuable transition between an early America where acculturation was not a major feature—i.e., the White majority tended to be a homogeneous culture, with no real attempt being made to integrate the sizeable minorities of Negroes or Native Americans—and the coming periods which, from an acculturational viewpoint, would feature many more modalities of individual choice. In other words The Melting Pot, while once a viable idea for some, became largely irrelevant.

American Life After The Melting Pot

In 1998 *The Washington Post* ran a series of articles entitled "The Myth of the Melting Pot." Referring to the period between 1880 and 1920, described in the previous chapter, it said at one point: "The United States is experiencing its second great wave of immigration, a movement of people that has profound implications for a society that by tradition pays homage to its immigrant roots at the same time it confronts complex and deeply ingrained ethnic and racial divisions. The immigrants of today come not from Europe but overwhelmingly from the still developing world of Asia and Latin America. They are driving a demographic shift . . . (that) . . . will severely test the premise of the fabled melting pot, the idea, so central to national identity that this country can transform people of every color and background into 'one America'."

How did this phenomenon look to those situated within this new immigrant wave? Let us listen to another kind of voice—that of Jorge Ramos, a distinguished Hispanic journalist writing at about that same time: "The melting pot dried up. We, the Hispanic community, did not (merge) into U.S. Society as other ethnic groups had before us; we did so in our own way. Hispanics have built their identity on cultural roots and origins that are different from those of the rest of the population. That sets us apart from all other immigrant groups in the history of The United States" (Ramos, 2000, Introduction, pp. xxix & xxx). Ramos continued by quoting well known Peruvian writer Mario Vargas Llosa: "It is the first time in history that an immigrant community has not had to go through the process of the melting pot which is that of conforming to the customs of the (primarily) English-speaking population in order to be recognized as Americans" (Ramos, 2000, Introduction, p. xxx).

What has happened in the years since these passages were writen? As noted above, immigration has slowed for all groups, including Hispanics. However, the second generation of immigrants from the 1990 wave—comprising those who were born here—is increasing in prominence. As I will discuss later, second and subsequent generation Hispanic and Far Eastern immigrants often have substantial exposure to modern information technology—which serves to give them the capability to separate from their traditional cultures when it suits their purpose. It has never been easier than it is right now for the descendants of any immigrant culture to resist the forces that led to the popularization of the idea of the one-size-fits-all Melting Pot.

Scholars Look at Acculturation

In this context of social process change it is useful to explore the scholarly literature in the field of acculturation study. It is generally accepted that the first serious thinking about acculturation came from the anthropological community. In 1936, Redfield, Linton and Herskovits wrote as follows: "Acculturation comprehends those phenomena which result when groups of individuals having different cultures come into continuous first-hand contact, with subsequent changes in the original culture patterns of either or both groups" (p. 149).

One point of significance here is the *direction* of change, which could go from either group to the other. This initial idea of *dual directionality* differs both in concept and in voice from later constructs which proceeded from frameworks made up of *"original culture"* and *"dominant culture"* or similar value laden descriptors. These conceptualize cultural change as being handed from a "main" cultural entity to a "subsidiary" one. Also of interest in the Redfield definition was the focus on *group*, rather than *individual*, change.

In the 1940s there was interest in how the establishment of European colonial empires affected the colonized indigenous peoples, again portraying a diad of cultures in a superior/inferior mode. In 1945 Hollowell wrote (referring to the period leading up to World War I): "As the expansion of European peoples continued to gain momentum . . . conditions were created that directly or indirectly forced native peoples to make all kinds of cultural readaptations for which they were totally unprepared. This was inevitable since the ultimate aim of European expansion was the colonization and economic exploitation of new regions, and the extension of sovereignty over the . . . people who lived in them" (Hollowell, 1945, p. 192).

Hollowell quotes earlier writing by Barnett in further denigrating societies that came to be colonized: ". . . the socially unadjusted or maladjusted, the suppressed and frustrated and those who have suffered a social displacement in their own society, more especially half-breeds, widows, orphans, invalids, rebels and chronic trouble makers have been in the vanguard of those accepting newly introduced patterns" (Barnett, 1941, p. 216).

Important at that time was the 1954 definition of acculturation issued by The (American) Social Science Research Council (SSRC). They described acculturation as: ". . . culture change that is initiated by the conjunction of two or more autonomous cultural systems. Its dynamics can be seen as the selective adaptation of value systems, the processes of integration and differentiation, the generation of developmental sequences and the operation of role determinants and personality factors" (p. 974).

Bearing in mind that the time-frame of the SSRC concept statement was prior to some important developments in the field that I will describe later, still it must be noted that this definition lacked an explicit position on either of the two issues of acculturation study that came to be considered primary: (1) W*hether acculturative change could be expected to go in one or both directions—directionality.* This positional vacuum on an issue that had been present since the work of Redfield et al. set up two different views of acculturation, which were debated for years. One side interpreted the SSRC statement as proclaiming acculturation as a one-way street. The other said it implied a two way street. (2) *Whether acculturation was a uni-dimensional or orthogonal (multi- dimensional) construct—dimensionality.* The multi-dimensional construct was based on the idea that development of more than one personality could go on within the same person at the same time.

During the period following the 1954 SSRC statement the terms *acculturation* and *assimilation* were often used interchangeably. However, by the mid-1960s the view that acculturation—mainly affecting the newer group on the scene (directionality)—progresses in a straight line fashion from a native state, through transitional states to a fully assimilated state (dimensionality) was considered the traditionalist view (See Spindler and Spindler, 1967, as noted by Trimble in Chun, Balls Organista and Marin, 2003, p. 6).

Starting in the mid-1960s Gordon began what was to become a series of different looks at acculturation and assimilation within the social sciences. Note that this search for new directions roughly corresponded in time to the 1965 Amendments to the Immigration Act of 1952, the Amendments comprising an event which marked the beginning of the surge of immigration from Latin America and Asia and the broadscale appearance in America of immigrants who embodied a different personality profile. Gordon (1964) formulated an alternative framework that distinguished between *behavioural assimilation*, which he equated to acculturation (meaning the extent to which the minority group has absorbed the cultural patterns of the host society, such as language, dress, diet, sport, art or religion) and *structural assimilation* (referring to the degree to which the minority group has become dispersed into the host culture—p. 140). In this dichotomy, acculturation was conceptualized as a subcategory of assimilation, rather than the other way around.

Following up Gordon's thinking, in 1974 Teske & Nelson put forth a different type of schema. They compared acculturation and assimilation as *overlapping processes*. Both were dynamic processes, fitting with either individual or group level analysis and derived from direct contact. Differences in their constructs included directionality (two way acculturation vs. one way assimilation), value change (required for assimilation but not acculturation) and presence of/acceptance by an outside reference group (also required for assimilation but not acculturation) (p. 365).

Paralleling Gordon's work, in 1967 Graves made an important contribution to the body of acculturation theory with his concept of *psychological acculturation*. Prior to this (even back to the previously cited work of Redfield et al some 30 years earlier) the context of acculturation study had been the group. Graves' thinking is summed up as follows (1967, p. 347): "The objective contact situation exists external to the minority group member, who must operate within it, and limits the amount of exposure to the dominant group and the type of opportunities open to him. These, in turn, may have a significant impact on the psychological beliefs and values which the minority group member develops." According to Kim and Abreu (2001, p. 396) there were several important elaborations on the idea of psychological acculturation. They cite Szapocznik et al (1978, p. 113) as characterizing psychological acculturation as comprising *behaviours* as well as values. They further cite Padilla as adding *cultural awareness* and *ethnic loyalty* as important elements of psychological acculturational beliefs.

The basic topography of acculturation was expanded and pretty much settled by the work of John Berry, covered in more detail in the next chapter. His distinctions derived initially from early ethnographic work preparatory to psychometric study with Aboriginal peoples in Australia and elsewhere (Sommerlad & Berry, 1970, p. 23). Berry's work integrated early anthropological investigation featuring contextual impacts on acculturating groups with the individually oriented psychological acculturation focus of Graves and others cited above. The idea of treating acculturation strategies as resultant from the intersection of two dimensions—one pertaining to the original culture and the other the new, host culture—developed during this period (Berry and Sam, 1997, p. 296).

Work by others in the late twentieth century expanded on the Berry foundation and focused once again on the two historic issues of acculturation—dimensionality and directionality. First, regarding dimensionality, Sanchez & Fernandez stated: "In support of the bi-dimensional approach, our results provided evidence for the independence of the two identification dimensions. That is, the individual's level of Hispanic identification was unrelated to his/her American identification . . ." (Sanchez and Fernandez, 1993, p. 664). Another of the important bridging studies dealing with uni-dimensionality vs. orthogonality was done in 1997 by Cuellar, Nyberg, Maldonado and Roberts. Looking at young Mexican-Americans they concluded that: "High Biculturals were unique in that they had both high ethnic identity and were highly oriented toward other ethnic groups" (p. 546).

In further developments, Suarez-Orozco (2001) pointed out that "assimilation and acculturation themes predict that change is 'directional, unilinear, nonreversible and continuous' . . . however this is not what occurs with immigrant populations. Ethnic or cultural groups select *portions* of a *dominant or contributing* culture that fit their original worldview and, at the same time, strive to retain vestiges of their traditional culture" (p. 7). Then, the Cuellar et al (plus other) results were taken by Phinney (2003) as a demonstration (at least for Hispanics) that ". . . ethnic identity does not diminish with greater orientation toward the host culture. Ethnic identity can remain strong without interfering with participation in the larger society" (p. 71).

Looking to broaden the idea, in 2000 Ryder, Alden and Pallhus wrote that: ". . . people exposed to two cultures, either through birth or through heritage, can incorporate, to varying degrees, two coexisting cultural identities. Furthermore, it does not seem to be the case that the old cultural identity necessarily diminishes while the new one grows; rather the two identities can vary independently. In short, a *bi-dimensional conception*, with independent heritage and mainstream dimensions of culture, appears to be far richer and more functional than the traditional uni-dimensional approach" (p. 63). Phinney (2003, p. 78) endorsed the more ethnically comprehensive construct, saying "Currently in the United States, members of non-European immigrant groups generally develop *bi-cultural identities*—that is they become American but also retain their (original) ethnic identity over time."

So, as of the end of the twentieth century, those favoring an orthogonal (multi-dimensional) acculturation construct—at least for immigrants in the more recently dominant flow groups (mainly Hispanics and Asians)—seemed clearly to have prevailed in that part of the overall American acculturation debate.

But what about directionality? A study on the directionality of change that I consider key was done by Richman, Gaviria, Flaherty, Birz and Wintrob in 1987. They discussed the possibility that the *dominant* or *donor* culture may undergo a change process influenced by aspects of the *newcomer* culture or acculturating group (p. 7). This thinking echoed and resurrected the original anthropological ideas of Redfield et al as to which group had influence on which (but still framed the argument in terms of the intrinsic assumption that the newer group was on a one-dimensional track). My own belief is that the directionality issue came to lose its relevance as it became obvious that late twentieth century main-stream American culture was, in fact, being heavily influenced by trends from immigrant groups, at least in domains such as entertainment and cuisine. For example, *The Encyclopedia of Latino Popular Culture* (Candelaria, 2004) lists 73 Latino actors who had gained fame and rec-ognition in The United States (e.g., Edward James Olmos, Emilio Estevez, Jennifer Lopez, et al p. xvi), 68 musicians and singers (e.g., Gloria Estefan, Ricky Martin, Mark Antony et al, p. xxiii) and 12 different dances (e.g., cha cha, meringue, mambo, et al, p. xix). Hispanic foods that had crossed over to mainstream American society included tacos, enchiladas, chili and other Mexican foods readily available in stores and capable of being served at home or in country-wide restaurant chains such as Taco Bell, On the Border, Chili's, El Pollo Loco and many others.For a time more salsa was sold in American supermarkets than ketchup, the latter being a classic American favorite condiment.

Another example of everyday American culture absorbing features from immigrants' cultures was the Japanese influence, which was readily apparent in these same genres. Probably the most visible of the cross-over foods was sushi. However, other Japanese dishes and specialty cook-ing approaches such as sashimi, soba noodles, ramen, tempura, teriyaki, sukiyaki and tepanyaki (the cooking style made popular by the Benihana chain of restaurants) were increasingly to be found. In entertainment, genres such as the manga (adult comic book, often dealing with mature subjects) and the anime form of filmed entertainment have been popular and have carved out distinct niches in the American arts and entertain-ment scene.

A final noteworthy aspect of the development of acculturation study was the movement around the end of the twentieth century to *measure acculturation*. Studies by Zane and Mack (2003, p. 53), Kim and Abreu (2001, p. 401) and The Antioch University Multicultural Center (2006, p. 1) each provide lists of scales that had been published in the social science literature. Integrating the lists shows that between 1978 and 2001 no fewer than forty-eight different "acculturation measuring" instruments had been developed. Of these measures, 42 were designed for use with a specific ethnic group (26 Hispanic, 10 Asian and 6 other ethnic). Only six were designed for broader use. In many cases the intended subject constituency was a sub-group (e.g., Mexicans, Chinese) or even a sub-sub-group (e.g., Chicano adolescents). This demonstrates a design paradox that is built into this kind of research. It is generally accepted that ethnographic work should occur at the beginning of cross-cultural studies—so as to ensure, for example, that the wording of questions makes sense to the subjects. Yet the more diligent the ethnographic work the less the utility of the instrument tends to be outside the group for which it was designed.

Most of the measures tended to be framed within the dimensionality issue only and therefore had limited relevance for directionality. Both Kim and Abreu and Zane and Mack showed a wide variation in specifically what was being focused on from one instrument to another, all in the name of acculturation. Both teams found ranges from 100% behaviours to 100% values. This leads me to agree with the following statement from Zane and Mack (p. 52): "It is questionable whether the measures are assessing the same acculturation phenomena . . . (as) there is a lack of content overlap even among measures that were designed to assess the same ethnic group." An appropriate analogy might come from the field of automobiles. A mechanic's garage, a body shop, a new car dealership and an auto driving school all have to do with cars—everyone involved in any of those industries could say "I am in the car business." Yet the activity content and skill requirements of the four businesses are quite different. What matters is what they do with the cars. This type of material, even if valid, would be of use mainly to academics or those from the clinical schools of psychology or psychiatry. Certainly such tools may be useful within these groups. But the empirical measurements are generally so limited, technical and complicated that there is little of practical value. One cannot understand where an ethnic immigrant is in terms of acculturative development and what one could reasonably expect his or her reactions to be in conversations or situations requiring some action.

Summing up this section, the decreasing belief in The Melting Pot as a broadly relevant acculturative construct and the increasingly sophisticated dialogue about acculturation among social scientists set the stage for important developments in the later part of the twentieth century. These will be discussed in more detail in Chapters THREE and FOUR.

Chapter THREE

The Emergent Bi-Cultural Personality

By the end of the twentieth century acculturation scholarship had advanced to the point where the two main historical questions had, in the views of many people, moved well along toward resolution. The original anthropological concept of Redfield et al (1936) that acculturation could affect both the original culture and the receiving culture seemed on balance to be accurate. Therefore it would be reasonable to expect at least some influence from each culture on the other—although the magnitude of the affects would, of course, not be exactly equal. Further there was a substantial body of research evidence and scholarly opinion that acculturation was a condition that could be analyzed on the basis of more than one dimension that could exist within the same individual at the same time—that it was a potentially *orthogonal* or multi-dimensional condition, as distinguished from earlier concepts of acculturation that pictured it as uni-dimensional (i.e., the acculturating individual was earlier thought to progress in a straight line fashion from embodiment of an original culture through various stages of acculturation to an end-state of assimilation). Therefore, based on the more advanced, orthogonal concept it was considered at least conceptually possible for immigrants to continue to embody personalities formed around their traditional cultures while forming new, separate personalities modeled on what was experienced in their new surroundings.

The original idea of acculturation as a phenomenon relevant to groups continued to be applicable. However, this conceptualization had been supplemented with the idea of *psychological acculturation*—i.e., adjustments by the individual, in response to contextual and sociological factors relevant to his (or her) new surroundings and cultures. These adjustments were not driven completely by external forces but had a direct relationship to individual factors brought along from the past.

There was at the same time, however, considerable semantic and conceptual confusion as to just what acculturation was. Values and behaviours were treated as if they were the same thing. And many different constructs were labeled acculturation—e.g., ethnic identity changes, knowledge and beliefs. Many felt the need for an overall analytical model to pull together concerns about original culture-relevant and new culture-relevant contextual and sociological factors involved in acculturation, and to show their interplay with the psychological set brought to the situation by the individual immigrant. There was a concurrent need to define the strategies available and chosen for acculturation purposes as well as a need for a way of understanding why a given immigrant chose the pattern he did. This kind of model would also be helpful in positioning acculturative phenomena and adjustment strategies within the wider context of the continual absorption of new realities, breakdown of boundaries, and re-formations of the self that pertained not only to immigrants but to all people.

The Berry Acculturational Model

One of the most significant developments in acculturation theory may be attributed to Dr. John Berry, a prominent cross-cultural psychologist from Canada. He has invested many years of scholarship in projects all over the world dealing with acculturation (see Berry & Sam, 1997; Berry, 2003). He is widely accepted as one of the top experts in this field and is often cited by others studying acculturative phenomena. It will be useful here to provide a summary of Berry's acculturation model. The following text points (and one chart) are taken from Berry's essay *Conceptual Approaches to Acculturation* (in Chun et al, 2002, pp. 17 and ff).

Berry deals broadly with individual and societal factors one must look at in coming to understand the acculturative process. He focuses heavily on strategies groups of individuals follow in working through how they will play the game of acculturation and how the receiving societies play their game of determining the treatment mode for "newcomers" or other minorities.

Berry divides individual adjustment into the categories of *psychological adjustment*—individual internal adaptation, similar to Graves' (1967) psychological acculturation—and *sociocultural adjustment* (factors that link the individual with the new culture). He also makes reference to changes in the host culture group that can be expected, stemming from contact with the newcomers (2003, p. 20).

Berry describes the background factors involved in a specific individual's choice of acculturation strategy as including the direct effects on him of the new culture, the adjustments being made to the new culture by the members of his original culture that form his relevant sub-group and finally the effects of that sub-group on the individual. Individual adjustments can be psychological, sociocultural, or both. Additionally, adjustments run the gamut from relatively simple behavioural adjustments to complex, difficult to achieve adjustments which can result in acculturative stress and serious psychological issues if not addressed. Also relevant are changes in the new culture coming from contact with the sub-group of original culture individuals.

Berry envisions two separate dimensions—one dealing with the original culture and the other dealing with the receiving culture. The *original culture dimension* runs between the condition of *Separation* and that of *Assimilation*. The dimension dealing with the new *host culture* runs between *Marginalization* and *Integration*. He describes the four conditions as follows (p. 24): *Separation*—individuals place a value on holding on to their original culture and at the same time wish to avoid interacting with others. *Assimilation*—individuals do not wish to maintain their (original) cultural identity and seek daily interaction with other cultures. *Marginalization*—individuals perceive little possibility and have little interest in cultural maintainance and at the same time have little interest in having relationships with others. *Integration*—Individuals have an interest in maintaining their original culture during daily interactions with other groups.

Berry continues his own discussion of acculturation strategies: "(My) portrayal of acculturation strategies was based on the assumption that nondominant groups and their individual members have the freedom to choose how they want to acculturate. This is, of course, not always the case" (2003, p. 24). He elaborates as follows: ". . . people in voluntary contact are more likely to seek greater participation . . . than those who are not in voluntary contact, such as refugees" (p. 30). Kim & Berry (1986, p. 159) add: "Those whose appearance makes them distinct from the dominant population may be less attracted by assimilation or be kept away by racism and discrimination."

Turning to other contextual factors Berry states (op cit, 2003): "Social ecology and vitality (i.e., sheer numbers of people in the group) . . . may increase the possibility of (and perhaps preference for) cultural maintenance . . . (additionally) . . . the positive or negative multicultural ideology encountered in daily interactions with members of the dominant society may reinforce certain preferences" (p. 30).

Berry incorporates into his overall acculturation model national and societal policies relative to immigrants to show how the everyday context for immigrant life could be affected by the intent of their adopted societies toward them. Just as the above-described part of the Berry model has four strategies for immigrant groups to choose from for acculturative adjustment purposes, Berry sees a roughly corresponding set of four national and societal policy approaches. Accordingly, the immigrant acculturation strategy of Separation (preferring interactions within one's own culture) would have as its national policy correlate *Segregation*—a policy such as was manifested in the late nineteenth and early twentieth centuries in The United States by the dominant white culture toward blacks—a policy which could tend to force the non-dominant group into a Separative or possibly Marginalized posture. The immigrant acculturation strategy of Assimilation (seeking interactions with the dominant group rather than with one's original culture group) would correspond in the national/societal part of the model to a *Melting Pot* construct, such as was discussed earlier as an idea popular with some parts of mainstream early twentieth century America even if it was only partially accurate with respect to the immigrants themselves. The Melting Pot societal idea would infer that distinguishing features of particular immigrant cultures would, over time, recede relative to mainstream characteristics—for example with respect to food, language and similar everyday domains. Marginalization, withdrawing from both one's own culture and that of the receiving society, would correspond to *Exclusion*—for example, episodes of attempted ethnic cleansing such as occurred in Hitler's Germany or present day Darfur, the objective of which was to eliminate a specifically targeted minority group. Finally, Berry's Integration strategy, in which individuals demonstrate an interest both in maintaining their original culture and having daily interactions with other groups, would correspond in Berry's thinking with *Multiculturalism*—the understanding of the society as essentially plural as in Canada. The following diagram is used by Berry to illustrate his acculturation model (ibid, 2003, p. 23):

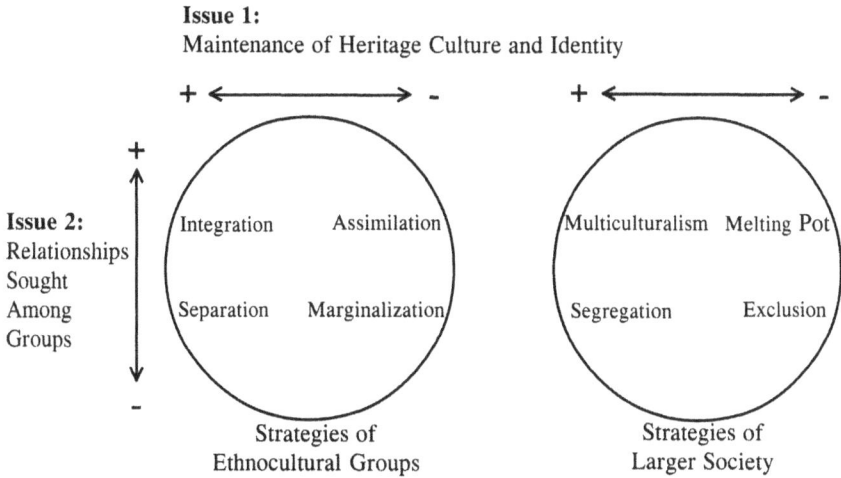

Issue 1:
Maintenance of Heritage Culture and Identity

+ ⟵———————⟶ -   + ⟵———————⟶ -

Issue 2:
Relationships
Sought
Among
Groups

| Integration | Assimilation |
| Separation | Marginalization |

| Multiculturalism | Melting Pot |
| Segregation | Exclusion |

Strategies of
Ethnocultural Groups

Strategies of
Larger Society

Four acculuration strategies based on two issue—
views of ethnocultural groups (*left*) and of larger society (*right*)

I find the mirror-like nature of the two parts of the Berry model, as illustrated above, provides an interesting visualization and starting point for an integrated understanding of acculturational development.

My concern in the balance of this chapter is with Berry's Integrative quadrant (upper left part of the left circle in the diagram above). For this is where the *bi-cultural personality* would reside if placed within the Berry model. The bi-cultural personality is a construct that many scholars feel is characteristic of many immigrants to America in the most recent wave—coming largely from Latin America and the Far East.

Bi-Culturality at the Individual Level: The ACES Framework

I view the Berry model of acculturation as a major accomplishment in relating constructs that had previously been studied in relative isolation and structuring the entirety into a web of relationships that is easy to understand. The two dimensions that connect Berry's four strategic acculturation quadrants give substance to the more abstract idea of "*or-*

thogonality" meaning multiple dimensionality (i.e., more than one relevant dimension can exist within the same individual at the same time). Moreover, the mirror-like four quadrants comprising strategic options for the *larger society* (on the right side of the model) give a *symmetry* to the system that I find helpful, while putting into a clear perspective just what is meant by terms such as *"contextual factors"* or *"environment"* and further enriching the idea of *"directionality."*

Yet the Berry model is, in my view, incomplete in some important respects. First, I believe that—while comprehensive in a sense—it is at the same time too simplistic, in that the end result is that the individual ends up in a defined, conceptually bounded state that ignores the larger *spectrum of influences* from other domains that introduce constant change and personal growth. For example, a Chinese immigrant with a more or less bounded personality may come to enjoy Mexican food, or learn to speak another language (or even a different dialect of Chinese so that he can communicate and relate to a broader spectrum of his own basic ethnicity), thereby transitioning from Separation to Integration Quadrants.

Another respect in which I believe the Berry model incomplete is that it stops short of placing the individual more *precisely* within the acculturation strategy quadrant that has been chosen. Consequently, using the model as a prism through which to view and understand an immigrant person one would only know as much about him as the group of which he is a member. The relevance of this shortfall, it seems to me, is that using only the Berry model by itself it is difficult to predict how a particular immigrant would react in conversations or serious dialogues, in attempts to persuade him/her of particular points or to get commitment to an action scenario. In essence the model might disregard the texture and richness of relationship that could be there.

Of course, it might be possible to utilize a set of empirical measurements to fill in the missing knowledge. However this course of action is both impractical and limited. To do it, a full list of available scales would need to be examined to see which one or ones were suitable—in the sense of matching the ethnography of the subject and the situation. This selection would still be biased by the researcher's stereotypes. Then the actual instrument would need to be acquired, administered and scored—an often complicated process. In my view, using empirical acculturation measurement scales is not an attractive option for developing a better understanding of the immigrant and his particular context. This presents an improvement opportunity.

In pursuit of this possibility I will put forward in the next sections an interpretive framework that I call *ACES*—an acronym for *Anchoring (A), Communication (C), Enjoyment (E) and Sensitivity (S)*. ACES utilizes subjective judgments on a few factors that I have found particularly important in both my professional and non-professional lives to establish the *degree* to which an individual, whether immigrant or not, has achieved *full bi-culturality*. Full bi-culturality is, for many, a desired condition in that it enables a richer and more articulated view of life—an important goal for many immigrants, as will be discussed in Chapter FOUR—and an ability to envision and evaluate more options for planning and action, thereby often enabling superior performance in an organizational setting. For example, in international business scenarios, such as large multinational corporations frequently encounter, managers who are having difficulty reaching full states—or at least advanced states—of bi-culturality could encounter difficulty making effective, culture-sensitive decisions in functions such as international product planning, marketing strategy, distribution analysis, sales force management, operational and organizational development, first line supervision of ongoing production operations or human resources. These are examples of domains where being able to construct a bi-cultural understanding of emergent and potential scenarios is key.

My own experiences in international business taught me that it is easy to misjudge the depth and breadth of an individual's real cultural understanding by overlooking important but less salient factors that could become decisive for success later. I have, on a number of occasions, had to decide between candidates for important international positions based on how well I thought the candidate would understand a prospective non-native posting when he got there. On one occasion I mistook a Japanese executive's proficiency with the English language for comprehensive understanding of the American culture, with less than optimum results. In fact, my own career was influenced by my own less than full bi-culturality as I chose to focus my Hispanic Marketing consulting practice on the US Hispanic Market rather than necessarily seeking client work in Latin America.

When I first started working on the formulation of ACES my intent was that it be an *example* of a way to further position immigrants in the Berry model's Integrative Quadrant so we can know them better quickly and easily. As it has developed I have recognized the usefulness of its principles not only with respect to immigrants but to others as well.

ACES can be used with a *broad range of people who are or wish to be bi-cultural* and are therefore psychologically located within Berry's *Integrative* quadrant (Berry, 2003, p. 24).

Exploring the ACES Interpretive Framework

ACES works within the context of the Berry model (and particularly with those who are situated in the Integrative quadrant) by bringing the analytical focus down to the level of the *individual*. ACES adds to the Berry model a dimension of subjective understanding of where individuals are with respect to *full accomplishment of the bi-cultural condition*. This understanding applies to a variety of situations. When applied in an international business setting for example, it allows for more informed judgments regarding assignments, training needs and strategic business opportunities. In a non-business setting, as when applied to immigrants (my original and continuing intent), it shows more clearly how the individual constructs life in America and gives clues as to how to relate to him, communicate with him and help him accomplish his objectives.

In the complete condition of *full bi-culturality* the individual should be able to relate to changes in contextual situations through *either* of the interpretive prisms built into his two personalities, *without excessive biases* coming into play emanating from the personality not operative at that time. Moreover, the fully bi-cultural person should be capable of moving back and forth between personalities easily and transparently— as would be required when analyzing a potential cross-cultural scenario from alternate viewpoints. He should be able to relate to others from either of his two component cultures as if he were *uni-cultural* in that culture—being fully able to communicate and understand communications, dialogues, nuances and context whether the operative culture at that time is his original culture or the newer, alternate culture.

Many immigrants to America have told me that it is possible after living here for a few years to have enough of a familiarity with the country to begin to think of themselves as bi-cultural, and in essence to self-select Berry's Integrative acculturation strategy quadrant, perhaps without knowing that they are doing so. Yet my observation is that there are *degrees of bi-culturality*. For example, a Russian woman—someone I consider very advanced in engineering areas and who speaks what sounds to me, a native American English speaker, to be impeccable English— told me that even after living in America for years she was still not able to pick up subtle but important nuances in domains like Americans' non-verbal communications, jokes in and out of the Boardroom where significance resides in being able to decipher different levels of meaning and metaphoric language in newspapers and other media requiring a deeper understanding of American culture. In other words, she is bi-cultural to a large but not complete degree.

The four factors of ACES have been distilled over many years of my own experience to represent what I believe are *important aspects of mastery of a culture*. Many people who have gone through normal socialization in a particular culture are already at high levels of A, C, E and S in that culture. However, *full bi-culturality* requires similar levels in a relevant second culture. ACES starts out with individuals who *want* to be bi-cultural and who have accomplished this to a greater or lesser degree—i.e., they have self-selected the Berry Integrative quadrant, whether they were aware of the construct or not, and made at least some progress toward the full bi-culturality condition. ACES, then, places them more specifically within the Berry Integrative Quadrant—yielding a more sophisticated understanding of their individual condition and corresponding keys as to how to communicate effectively with them and help them move toward a greater degree of bi-culturality should they wish to do so.

ACES is based on my own synthesis of key factors. Certainly there could be other frameworks, for the Berry Integrative Quadrant as well as for other quadrants or other models. However, my years of organizational experience give me confidence that ACES is at least one valuable tool. ACES is essentially subjective and makes no pretense of having the high powered statistical validity that would allow use of correlational techniques. Rather it is a way of speaking a different language about relationships with immigrants and others—a language rooted in qualitative understanding of basically qualitative demands and a qualitative adjustment process.

What is ACES?

I'll initiate discussion of my ideas about ACES by explaining what I mean by each component and giving for each a brief illustrative example showing what an immigrant to America might consider doing to help establish a fully bi-cultural condition with his original ethnicity as one component and his new American persona as the other.

The first of the four ACES factors is *Anchoring (A)*. I intend this to mean the connection to a culture that initially comes from knowledge about it—understanding the nature of the society, its history, its laws, geography, economics, and place in the world to at least the level that should be expected of a reasonably intelligent, well informed citizen—for example, a university graduate. Additionally anchoring comprehends the ability to appreciate and internalize these inputs—to the point where one can act out the game of life in that culture in a way similar to those who are native to it. Someone who wishes to be *fully bi-cultural* must demonstrate that he/she is at that level with respect to both cultures.

For example, an English immigrant might want to study the development of American law and government to understand differences compared to corresponding old English constructs from which the American versions descended. This would serve both to strengthen anchoring with America through more detailed understanding and lend additional perspective to pre-existent anchoring with England.

The next ACES component is *Communication (C)*. Here I am referring to the ability to speak, read and write a language well enough that one can engage in dialogue using not only standard language but well known slang and metaphoric terms to the level where other people who might be involved in the dialogue *do not* feel compelled to choose their words carefully—avoiding more complex or specialized words that might convey a more sophisticated meaning. Here again, most people would more or less automatically have this ability with respect to their own culture. But getting to that level in the second culture is not always easy. I am not talking about having accented speech but about the real level of fluency that is behind it.

As an example, consider a Chinese immigrant who, in addition to learning what he could in the classroom about speaking English, sought out Americans for conversation, asking them to please not simplify their phraseology for his sake. This would serve to increase familiarity with sounds from the English language that are not present in Chinese (such as l and r), assure practice with verb tenses that are missing in Chinese and introduce commonly used slang terms from colloquial English that are frequently encountered in everyday life.

The third component is *Enjoyment* (E). Most people have typical activities that they enjoy in their own culture such as theatrical entertainment, parties and sports. The person who aspires to full bi-culturality needs to learn to genuinely enjoy the typical leisure activities of the alternate culture as well and be able to adapt smoothly to different ways the alternate culture approaches activities that are common to both.

Consider an immigrant from Russia for whom "a night out at the theatre" comprised going to the opera, ballet or other classical pursuits. Such a person could go to stage plays (such as Broadway shows) in the musical or comedy genres to gain an understanding and appreciation for the types of theatrical experiences enjoyed by many Americans, so that he could more easily relate to them when that is called for.

The final component of ACES is *Sensitivity (S)*. This means understanding the subtle cultural nuances that often change the meaning of what is said or done, such as body language and other forms of nonverbal communication, as well as metaphors and other cultural cues that are embedded in what people say and do that alter or extend their intended meaning relative to what is apparent on the surface.

In the Japanese culture there is a mode of speaking called *tate mai*. This prototypically Japanese concept means saying or doing things either because they are expected or because not to do them would cause unwanted confrontation. Often inaccurate or potentially misleading information or response is given out in conversations and most Japanese understand from context that the information should be ignored. In American society this would be considered lying, something many Americans would prefer not to do personally or even witness being done by others. So Japanese immigrants sometimes need to try to move toward understanding that overt differences of opinion are acceptable in America—are, in fact, a part of many Americans' everyday outlooks—and that open interpersonal confrontation is not necessarily the negative condition that it often can be in Japan.

Establishing Individual Position Using ACES

ACES is not intended to be used in large scale quantitative research efforts requiring regression or other similar types of statistical analytic work. Nevertheless, I believe it would be useful to have some way of relating immigrant (or other) individuals wishing to be fully bi-cultural to each other in terms of the degree to which they have achieved their objective. In this section, I will offer some thoughts in that direction.

Returning to the basic concept of ACES and its relationship to the condition of full bi-culturality, to achieve full bi-culturality an individual would need to exhibit high levels of performance in *both* cultures on *each* of the four dimensions of ACES. To allow at least some informal measurement I will stipulate 3 positions for each dimension—A, C, E and S: a position of *3* would mean that the individual was judged to have *full performance capability* on the dimension in *both cultures* (e.g., A = 3 would mean that the individual was fully anchored, as defined above, in both cultures). A position of 2 would indicate that full performance capability was evidenced with respect to *one culture but not the other* (e.g., C = 2 would mean that the person had complete communications command in one culture's language—in most cases this would be his own—but that command in the other language was either deficient or missing). A position of *1* would mean that full performance was *not evidenced in either culture* (e.g., S = 1 would mean that the person was not highly sensitive to nuances in either culture—even his own). A fully bi-cultural person would have a *full bi-culturality rating (FBR)* of 12—earning the maximum of three points on each of the four relevant dimensions (A, C, E and S).

ACES can be used either for self-evaluation (S) or for the evaluation of others (O), based on personal knowledge and/or the observation of behaviors and performance. Putting these together would allow comparisons of S ratings with O ratings or for different others' ratings of the same person to be compared to build up a picture of how a fully bi-cultural S is seen by the various Os in his particular reference group.

As an example, I will evaluate myself with respect to *the diad American and Hispanic*. Then, in the next section I will present composite narratives constructed from multiple discussions with immigrants from two different cultures—all of whom considered themselves at least at one point to be bi-cultural but, as ACES will show, only some of whom have actually achieved full bi-culturality.

I give myself an (S) FBR of 10 (3, 2, 2, 3) out of a possible 12. This is detailed as follows—I believe myself to be fully anchored (A) in both American and Hispanic cultures, including not only Mexico, where many US Hispanic immigrants come from, but other Latin countries as well. Therefore my self-rating on this dimension is 3. I read, write and speak English with native language fluency. Additionally, I can read and write Spanish with almost the same degree of fluency. When I speak to other Spanish-literate people in Spanish they can usually understand what I am saying. However, I sometimes have a problem understanding when others speak in Spanish to me, particularly if they are using regionally nuanced Spanish that I am not completely familiar with or speak too quickly.

So, falling short of full capability in that one respect I earn a 2 for Communication (C). I believe that I have a range of activities I enjoy in America that is similar to most Americans. However, many Hispanic leisure time activities are quite opaque to me. Since I demonstrated full capability in only one of the two cultures I earn a 2 for Enjoyment (E). Finally, despite not understanding some types of Hispanic games and leisure activities, still I believe I have at least an average (for Hispanics) understanding of the culturally nuanced areas of Hispanic life. Accordingly I rate myself as 3 on Sensitivity (S). My FBR is $(3 + 2 + 2 + 3)$ = 10 out of a possible 12.

As the illustration above shows, I am not fully bi-cultural in the diad American-Hispanic. This has had a career impact in the sense that I have tried to avoid situations where critical information was expected to be delivered to me in spoken Spanish only. To more closely approach full bi-culturality I know what I would need to do, at least isolating the general areas where improvement was needed. If others were to rate me in a similar fashion they could know this as well. If I could achieve full bi-culturality I would be able to add to my current ability to function at the level of a competent uni-cultural person in the American culture a similar level of ability in the Hispanic culture. I would be able to move back and forth between the two cultures more completely and transparently than I can right now. Finally, my capability for handling complex, culturally sensitive (American-Hispanic) scenarios in business and in life would improve—i.e., I would be capable of more informed, more sophisticated decisions and, by virtue of this, become more valuable not only to a multi-national corporation but to myself.

Additional Dimensions for ACES

Earlier in this Chapter I criticized the Berry Model on several grounds. I felt that the spaces in the Berry quadrants were too large to detect small but conceivably significant changes in an individual's position representing movements toward his original culture, toward his new culture or both. An additional criticism was that the individual ends up in a conceptually bounded state that does not recognize influences that serve to introduce constant change and personal growth. I introduced the ACES framework—built on four factors which my experience indicated were important for accomplishing the condition of bi-culturality—as a way to position an individual more precisely in Berry's Integrative quadrant. I also introduced a way of ascertaining the individual's degree of success in achieving the fully bi-cultural condition where he was capable of moving back and forth freely and seamlessly between his two relevant cultures, acting in each as if uni-cultural in that culture. To accomplish the fully bi-cultural condition the individual would need to demonstrate, or be considered able to demonstrate, full capability with respect to each of the four ACES dimensions in both of the cultures being reviewed. Chapter FOUR will contain constructed case examples of individuals who did and did not succeed in accomplishing this advanced condition.

If one were looking for ways to criticize ACES, as described so far, it could be said that ACES is too narrowly focused in that the quantitative positioning described above results in a determination that the individual is or is not fully bi-cultural, with that end condition reached by factor bi-culturality achieved on each of the four basic ACES components. Those who are determined not to be fully bi-cultural are left with an indication of the particular ACES dimension or dimensions where additional capability needs to be demonstrated. However for some applications additional information might be helpful. Additionally, the same criticism of not being flexible enough to measure movement over time that I levied against the Berry model could be leveled against ACES, as so far described. In anticipation of these criticisms I will point out that there could be other ways of reviewing an individual's position through the ACES framework that might serve these particular ends.

One example, relating to the procedure in the section above, might concern situations where the individual was rated as 2—fully capable in one of the two cultures but not the other. If more detail was desired this intermediate category (between 3 meaning capable in both cultures and 1 meaning not capable in either culture) could be expanded through stipulation of the *culture where the shortfall occurs* and the *degree or nature of the shortfall*. Referring back to my own self-rating, given above, for the diad American-Hispanic, I rated only a 2 in Communication (C), meaning that I was fully capable in one language but not fully capable in the other. To extend the system I might be rated in more detail on Communication (C) with factors pointing to Spanish as being the location of deficiency and perhaps b (out of a possible range of a, b and c) as showing how close I was to full accomplishment—resulting in a rating of 2/S/b or something similar in this example. An alternative might be to signal the *nature* of the deficiency rather than the *degree*. To continue with the example, a four point dimension might be used—for this application possibly w-z, where w = speaking, x = understanding speech, y = reading and z = writing. Thus, in this approach, my Communication (C) rating might be 2/S/x, indicating with greater precision that my weakness in the area was in understanding spoken Spanish. Additionally a combination of these two approaches could be designed.

Addressing the issue of individual change over time, sequential ACES ratings could be done at different times and the results compared to yield a picture of how the individual had changed. Continuing with the same example, if I were to enroll in an intensive one month course in understanding spoken Spanish to improve my one area of weakness I might possibly get a *pair* of ACES Communication (C) ratings that might look like this:

$$18/9/07/S/2/x-18/10/07/S/3$$

meaning that between the date this is being written (18 September 2007) and one month later (18 October 2007) I had eliminated the area of deficiency and gone to a condition of full Communication (C) capability in both languages, at least qualifying me for full bi-culturality in the Communication (C) dimension.

My purpose in this section has been to point out that ACES concepts could fit with other ways of scoring to accomplish objectives other than the determination of whether the individual was or was not fully bi-cultural. To avoid excess complexity I will in the balance of this book utilize the original rating system, oriented only to determination of full bi-culturality. In Chapter FOUR I will examine Hispanic and Japanese immigrants not from a theoretical viewpoint but in terms of the actual experiences they are having in America. The underlying question I will be dealing with is whether individuals from at least these two seemingly dissimilar original cultures can, with equal ease, develop the full bi-culturality condition in America. After that, in Chapter FIVE I will examine the Muslim immigrant culture and review what acculturational adjustment often means for them.

Chapter FOUR

Bi-culturality—The American Game of Hispanic and Asian Immigrants

In this Chapter I will move from treating Bi-culturality as a theoretical construct to examining it as a way some immigrants play the game of life in America. To do this I will start with the words of Phinney (2003, p. 78) quoted earlier in Chapter TWO: "Currently in the United States, members of non-European immigrant groups generally develop *bi-cultural identities*—that is they become American but also retain their (original) ethnic identity over time." In this and the next chapter I will examine how well Phinney's capsulization really fits with characteristics of groups from several different non-European original cultures now living in America. Additionally, in this chapter it will be helpful to explore whether it seems easier for some groups than for others, or for some individuals within the same group compared to others in that group, to achieve the condition of *full bi-culturality*—an idea introduced and developed in Chapter THREE. The present chapter will deal with bi-culturality among those with similar experiences—blending these together into fictitious but realistic characters—Hispanic and Asian immigrants, groups known to me from substantial personal experience. I will first look at American Hispanic immigrants through the writings of prominent scholars, supplementing these with my own observations. Then I will provide narratives—three Hispanic and two Japanese—constructed in each case from parts of conversations I have had with a number of people I know from that ethnicity who have had bi-cultural characters. In this way I will try to highlight in a dramatic fashion the conditions of these people while respecting their privacy. The composite individuals (as well as those real people the composites are based on) will all be individuals who started out intending to be Bi-Cultural but, as we will see, not always succeeding. Finally I will examine the objective of achieving full bi-culturality from the viewpoints of the two different cultures, showing similarities and differences in the obstacles that must be overcome. Chapter FIVE will discuss modes of adjustment among Muslim immigrant individuals.

The Hispanic Culture in America

Dr. Felipe Korzenny, a professor at Florida State University, is one of America's top experts on Hispanic immigrants and the culture they have developed here. Korzenny (2004) reviews the Berry acculturative model, granting it acceptance as a legitimate way of constructing reality for Hispanics. He summarizes Hispanics' current relationship to the model as follows:

> Generally, these days, Hispanics in the United States tend to either integrate (become bi-cultural) or remain separate but few seem to assimilate or to remain marginalized . . . Acculturated (integrated) individuals . . . are people who can navigate between the Hispanic and Anglo (non-Hispanic—phrase in parens mine) cultures . . . they have a more ample repertoire of behaviours available to them. . . . A tendency toward acculturation or bi-culturality is now the strongest emotional objective most frequently endorsed by Hispanics. Those who are relatively new to the United States understand the need to learn the second culture. Those who in the past had abandoned their Hispanic orientation are now reclaiming it themselves or through their children. That is because it is now a positive experience, in general, to be Hispanic in the United States. Despite remnant prejudice and discrimination, the overall balance of Hispanic experience in the United States is now more positive than it had been at other points in time. (p. 135)

Looking into the future Korzenny adds: "Hispanics will likely preserve their cultural roots due to the pride and desirability of the Spanish language and Hispanic culture in the United States. Thus, instead of assimilation, bi-cultural acculturation is more likely to take place" (ibid, p. 40). He continues: "In many ways this quadrant (referring to Berry's Integration—reference in parens mine) represents what the bulk of Hispanics will be in the future" (ibid, p. 140).

Consistent with this position Stephen Palacios, a researcher with Cheskin, Inc.—a company that has done extensive psycho-social research and consulting among US Hispanics—described their results as follows: "Cheskin has based its view that Hispanics are seeking to be bi-cultural on many of our attitude and behavior studies. For example, we have done three waves of national studies with Yankelovich and have consistently found an expressed interest in becoming bi-cultural both from less acculturated and by assimilated Hispanics—retroacculturating" (see Footnote 4.1).

What does it mean for a Hispanic to become Bi-Cultural? In 1991, well known Hispanic market researcher Isabel Valdes, drawing on earlier work of U. Bronfenbrenner (1979) and C. J. Falicov (1988) designed the following summary table, to show how the traditional values of a Hispanic working class family in America differed from those of a modern Anglo (not Hispanic) family (see Footnote 4.2).

Table 4.1: Comparison of Hispanic and Anglo Values

	Hispanic	**Anglo**
What is important	Family relationships	Individual achievement
Self perception	Family, group	Individual
Orientation	Relationships	Tasks
Families	Defined roles, age important	Democratic
Children	Dependent	Independent
Extended kin	Inclusive	Exclusive
Interactions	Complementary	Symmetrical
Physical closeness	High touch	More distant
Emotions	Show	Hide
Valued	Social background	Skills
Institutions	Believe unreliable	Believe reliable
Authority figures	Respected	Often questioned
Fate	Yes	No
Personal differences	Stressed, respected	Minimized
Service preference	Personalized	Efficient
Time	Relaxed	Scheduled
Fashion	Sensitive	Relaxed

This comparison might suggest that a Hispanic who wants to pursue a Bi-Cultural lifestyle needs to do more than just change to a different language when the situation requires. A Hispanic who moves into Bi-Cultural space must be able to change personas, literally flipping a switch to change one broad array of personal traits and value orientations to another. Is this possible? My own personal experience has largely been with Bi-Cultural Hispanics. I have done business with them, made presentations to and with them, dined with them, spent many an evening in deep philosophical discourse with them—many of these occasions in group situations involving a number of Hispanics. Based on this I believe that it is not difficult for Hispanics to move back and forth between personas that are fundamentally different. To recap briefly, Korzenny reviewed the Berry model of acculturation and opined that Integration was the Quadrant most American Hispanics prefer. Analysis of what is really needed to exist in bi-cultural space indicates that it appears difficult on the surface but is, in reality, readily accomplished by Hispanics. Korzenny adds that some Hispanics prefer Separation but that few choose either Assimilation or Marginality.

Integration as an Acculturation Strategy

Why would Hispanics gravitate toward integration as an acculturation strategy? Korzenny tells us (ibid): "The best of both worlds describes the position of those (Hispanic immigrants) who acculturate (become bi-cultural). They have the opportunity to select attributes of both cultures that they enjoy. Those who acculturate, as opposed to assimilate, have a more complex view on life" (p. 136).

In my own view, one major reason for the preference for integration involves the potential for improvement of finances through use of bi-lingual capability. To illustrate this point, many times in the past I made tutorial presentations about The US Hispanic Market. I often began these with a question. I provided as background information that there was a company in Los Angeles called The Lexicon School of Languages. This business sold very elaborate Learn English kits that were extremely expensive. Purchase normally required the use of installment financing, which was provided by the company. The target customer was a poor, recently arrived Hispanic (probably Mexican) with little money and no credit history. The question I asked the class was how many thought the company would be successful. Usually no one raised his hand. Then I asked how many thought the company would be a complete failure. Then usually everyone raised their hands. At that point I took off the covers and told the class that The Lexicon School of Languages was one of the most successful enterprises serving the US Hispanic Market. If their advertising is examined it is found to be aimed at working class Hispanics offering improved English ability as the means to the end of a better paying job and a better life in America. The success story of this one company, while certainly not conclusive of anything, does in my mind demonstrate the attraction of American economic opportunity for Hispanics. So why do we not see more Hispanic Assimilation?

Social philosophers such as Jorge Ramos, quoted earlier, might say this is because of the differences and enduring appeal of the Hispanic culture. Certainly there could be some validity to this argument. Yet I remain somewhat skeptical. My personal belief is that the key ingredient is the substantial infrastructure of Spanish language media readily and inexpensively available in the US. To quote Korzenny again (ibid):

> Univision, Telemundo (large Spanish language broadcast tv networks—material in parens mine), radio networks, newspapers and magazines have been dedicated to reach the Hispanic Market for a long time. The spectrum of media outlets has been dramatically expanded over the last few years and consolidation has also played a role. Now there are (cable tv channels such as Galavision and—material in parens mine) specialized internet channels like AOL Latino, Terra Nova Networks and Yahoo en Espanol that also facilitate targeting in the virtual interactive world. Notable new broadcast media channels include Mun2, Telefutura, and Azteca America." (p. 24)

In print there are many new successful offerings as well, such as *People en Espanol* and *Latina Magazine.*

I believe that the real significance of this vast Spanish language media infrastructure is that it is not necessary for Hispanics to let their original culture erode when they come to America and move up the largely English speaking economic ladder. They can easily have existences in both worlds. Moreover, as pointed out in Chapter ONE, the Hispanic segment of America is increasingly made up of second generation Hispanics, born here, who have a natural affinity for Bi-culturality by virtue of having one foot in each culture. Yet,as Korzenny has also mentioned, some Hispanics (a minority within a minority that is further declining in numbers and importance) gravitate toward Separation. The Spanish media infrastructure just discussed relative to Integration also supports those who choose Separation. However I believe there is more to the phenomenon than that. In some cases the Hispanic individual may not yet have learned to speak English well enough to feel comfortable in the mainstream culture (and may or may not ever be able to do so). In other cases the person's physical appearance, together with the likelihood of prejudice and discrimination, may cause the individual to steer away from the mainstream and seek to maintain traditional cultural relationships. Some individuals may also be undocumented and/or be living with friends or family members who are undocumented. Because of the risk of legal action or deportation such individuals usually shy away from excessive participation in mainstream activities.

Beyond that, many Hispanics come to the US with a constructed sense of inferiority that dates back to the days of Spanish colonial rule. This is difficult to overcome and introduces awkwardness into possible relationships with Anglos. Here are the words of Lionel Sosa—a highly regarded Hispanic advertising executive and Latino social critic (1999):

> The Spanish taught us subservience in the name of good manners. . . . It didn't stop there. If we questioned their ways we were referred to *their* Spanish priests who 'in the name of God' set us straight. "To be poor" they preached "is to deserve heaven. To be rich is to deserve hell." It is good to suffer in this life because in the next life you will find an eternal reward. . . . The way I see it, the Spanish conquerors deliberately created an oppressed underclass whose collective psyche became rooted in passivity and underachievement (p. 2). . . . We do not come from a puritan tradition, and so do not share the overachieving ethic it engendered. Our roots, like the African-Americans' lie in slavery, so we expect to earn our living by the sweat of our brow and the muscle in our back. . . . (p. 20)

Sometimes the Hispanic sees commercial advantages accruing from the perception by other Hispanics that he/she remains mostly Hispanic. Or possibly it was never the Hispanic immigrant's objective to stay in The United States long term. Thus, in some cases, substantial contact with mainstream America is unnecessary.

Bi-Cultural American Immigrant Experiences

As an American I have been privileged to have had extensive contact with many individuals from both Hispanic and Japanese backgrounds. In the former case, a business I ran for many years dealt largely with consulting to companies who wished to know more about Hispanics so as to pursue The US Hispanic Market in a strategically appropriate way. In the latter case, I lived in Japan for some time, married a Japanese woman and still have extensive dealings in that country and with its people. In this section I am going to provide narratives I have constructed—three Hispanic and two Japanese using composite characters made up from many of that ethnicity that I have known who have had similar experiences. I do this not only to preserve the privacy of individuals but also to provide more interesting narratives. In all cases the individuals started out with the intent of becoming *fully Bi-Cultural,* as I have described this condition earlier—i.e., able to perform fully in each culture as if uni-cultural in that culture with respect to each of Anchoring (A), Communications (C), Enjoyment (E) and Sensitivity (S). However some achieved this objective as a permanent condition, others did not. Within each narrative I will relate the character to ACES ratings and tell why each one fared as he or she did.

The Hispanic Narratives

This section will provide three narratives. The characters are technically fictitious but are, in fact, composites of many real people of Hispanic ethnicity who have had similar experiences. Ricardo, as I will call him, and Alfredo came from different Latino backgrounds but both succeeded in eventually becoming fully Bi-Cultural. The character Ramon started out with the intent to become fully Bi-Cultural but found that, for him, the more fulfilling choice was to return to his native culture and live a life of Separation in America—trading on his successful history as someone who kept a pure Hispanic persona.

Ricardo's Story

Ricardo grew up in an upper class Mexican family with homes in Mexico City and in the countryside. His father was a lawyer with extensive political connections in the Mexican government. His mother pursued charity work. He has an older brother and two younger sisters. While the family enjoyed the advantages of being at top levels in a socially stratified society, at the same time they felt some compassion for the poor and disadvantaged, of which there were many in Mexico.

Ricardo's father often traveled to The United States on business, taking his sons along when they were old enough and the entire family sometimes enjoyed holidays in America. On such trips, Ricardo's father often pointed out that, in America, status usually had to be earned rather than develop because of inherited social position as often tended to be the case in Mexico. Moreover, he tried to pass along the value that there is an important measure of self-respect that comes from earning a position in society, and that if the individual comes from a background where it is not necessary for him to work then the actual orientation to hard work is especially valuable. His role model was John F. Kennedy, former President of the United States.

Like other children from wealthy Mexican families Ricardo attended elite private Catholic schools. Of course these stressed the value of maintaining serious connection to the Catholic Church. They also stressed the importance of enjoying and preserving the Mexican culture—the Spanish language with its Mexican nuances, Mexican food, holidays, related traditions and the social system. English language study was offered as an elective and almost all students chose to study it. This led Ricardo to think that, perhaps underneath the love of Mexico that was an overt value at the school, many students secretly savoured a future life in America.

When Ricardo was 16 years old his older brother went to college in America—a large school in the Midwest part of the country. Keeping in touch with the family, he complained about the cold Winters but enjoyed the freedom from socially stratified life. There weren't many expectations for him emanating from American society. He felt that he was free to become whatever he could and wanted to be. When he returned home for school holidays he seemed to Ricardo a different person—more worldly and able to explain in greater depth and with more objectivity than before the differences between American and Mexican societies. This type of worldliness was new for Ricardo, whose views had previously been largely appropriated from his father. Today Ricardo's brother is a successful lawyer in Chicago.

As he approached the age where he too would soon need to apply to college Ricardo began thinking about building a Bi-Cultural life in America, taking on the characteristics of an American while at the same time maintaining a fundamental Mexican self-concept, maintaining close ties to his family (parents and two sisters) still in Mexico and to his brother.

Ricardo chose and was admitted to a prestigious engineering school in the Eastern part of The United States. After graduating with honours he went on to earn a masters degree in engineering. After that he continued his studies at a well known Eastern Business School, specializing in finance, mergers and acquisitions. In graduate school he met his wife, an attractive Russian. In time they were married and had one child, a daughter, whom they strived to raise as an American but with deep understandings of the different heritages mixed inside of her from her two parents.

Ricardo went on to have an excellent career, settling into the niche of buying and selling companies in Latin America for a New York based investment banking firm. Now in his late 30s, he travels much of the time—sometimes to Mexico and sometimes to other places in Latin America.

He is anchored in both societies, speaks both languages perfectly, enjoys the pleasures of each society while remaining sensitive to the nuances of life in each place. This composite person would be rated an ACES 12—fully Bi-Cultural.

Alfredo's Story

As Cuba began the year 1959 the Garcia family would, each night, huddle around the radio listening to the news of Fidel Castro and his rebel army advancing, moving closer and closer to Havana. Over a morning cup of Cuban coffee the next day Senora Garcia would chat with neighbors about what it would really mean if Castro was successful in overthrowing the Batista dictatorship then in power. Most of the neighbors talked of a socialist paradise they imagined being just around the corner, where wealth would be shared by all—not just those connected with "American capitalists and other foreign elements" as one neighbor put it—and the government would be kinder and treat everyone the same. But Senora Garcia suspected that the reality to come would not correspond so closely to this Utopian picture. Senora Garcia was largely right.

The new Castro regime brought with it repressive measures that were for many worse than what the people of Cuba had experienced before, as those suspected of actual or potential disloyalty to the revolution were systematically brought in, questioned and often incarcerated. Nevertheless a resistance movement was forming—one that had appeal to the older Garcia children. Alfredo, one of five, was at age twelve really too young to understand the situation completely. But he had listened to quiet family dinner conversation over the last few months as his father detailed the unfolding of a plan to purchase a boat and keep it hidden but ready for exit from Cuba at a moment's notice if needed. One night that moment arrived, as Alfredo's father rushed in before dinner telling of an arrest warrant that he had learned had been issued for Alfredo's sister, the eldest of the Garcia children. He told the family to leave everything, including the food on the table, pick up those precious things they could carry and follow him. They were leaving Cuba.

The escape and sea voyage to Miami had been well planned and proceeded according to that plan—perilous but with precautions well thought out in advance. The Garcias had alerted family members who had preceded them to America that they would probably also make the journey sometime soon. These relatives were ready to welcome the Garcias into their homes. After a time the Garcias began to adjust to their new surroundings and their legal status clarified. Sr. Garcia found work, they rented a home and settled into a routine.

Alfredo initially knew very little English. But he worked hard, picking up what he could from special school classes, schoolmates, American media and books. Within about a year he could more or less understand what was being discussed in English in school and around him. As time went on he became more and more fluent. By the time Alfredo was 18 years old the family was firmly established financially and Alfredo could look ahead to college. He applied to and was accepted at a highly ranked American university. Following this there was law school. Finally a business degree. He was ready to go to work.

Today Alfredo is a highly successful businessman. He has maintained his anchoring to Cuba through friends he made in school that he is still in touch with. He speaks both languages perfectly, enjoys social functions with Anglos (non-Hispanics) as well as his Cuban and other Hispanic friends and maintains an awareness of the nuances of life in both cultures. Alfredo earns an ACES 12, he is fully Bi-Cultural.

Ramon's Story

Ramon is now in his late 50s. He is a naturalized Argentine-American living in Los Angeles. He had a difficult youth, more or less estranged from his parents and growing up in the environment of a strict boarding school run by priests.

Trained at university as an economist he was on his way to a solid but limited position in Argentina. As he tells it, Argentine society is highly stratified. At one point he said: "*With a last name like mine you have a permanent position reserved for you in the underclass."* He felt that this was true no matter how intelligent or resourceful he was. He married and had three children, always thinking of moving to America. Finally, as he was approaching middle age, he got his chance—he could come to America to get an advanced degree and find a way to stay here to pursue opportunities he felt he wouldn't have if he stayed in his native land. After a time he brought his family up to America from Argentina. In America they had one additional child.

During his early years in America his days were divided into two parts. He worked during the day and went to school at night. During the day he followed the traditional Hispanic immigrant's career path. He began as a construction worker, then was hired for a sales position in a furniture store serving mostly Hispanic clientele but also some Anglos (non-Hispanics) who lived in the area. His marketing talent soon moved him into the fast growing field of Spanish language television and tele-communications, mainly marketing these media to Anglos. In my view, this sequence was significant in that Ramon was drawn increasingly into a bi-lingual, bi-cultural world where everyday interactions included some that were conducted in English and required higher levels of knowledge of the American culture.

He taught Beginning English as a Second Language (BESL) at university level some nights, other nights taking more advanced ESL classes himself. He began studying industrial management. All throughout this period Ramon believed himself to be moving further and further along on the road to Bi-culturality. His English was getting stronger, although he was far from being completely fluent. He felt he had learned a great deal about America from just living here for a substantial amount of time and through the insightful remarks of his management professors. On the other hand, his wife Juana spoke almost no English and maintained most of their Argentinian traditions at home. His children, mostly grown now, continued to orient toward Ramon in the deferent way they had when younger and living in Argentina. Further, Ramon never felt comfortable in social situations with English speaking Americans. He and Juana chose to socialize only with Hispanics, where cultural nuances came more naturally to them.

Several years ago Ramon began to encounter business problems. He became involved in the possible sale of a large, attractive Hispanic owned and operated business to Anglo financiers. After a great deal of effort and money had been expended the deal collapsed. Then Ramon formed a group with some of the original operators of the Hispanic business and attempted to start a similar one on a venture basis. This effort also failed. This sequence caused Ramon to re-think his strategy for continuation in America. Perhaps he had really not understood the institutional or personal situations on either side (particularly the American side) as well as he thought he had. Perhaps it was time to withdraw from bi-culturality as a main intended strategy and channel his full efforts into being successful within a basic strategy of Separation. After all, looking back on what he had done so far, he concluded that being a clever, resourceful Hispanic had been the one trait that had energized his success in America. Ramon is an example of a person who can gain from choosing the Seperation strategy in that there is value to him in some other Hispanics relating to him as "still Hispanic." His opportunity came soon. He was recruited by a financial services company that mainly sold insurance to US Hispanics, using advertising, telemarketing and other direct-to-consumer tactics phrased in Spanish. He has been very successful in this new role and has no immediate plans to change course.

The Japanese Narratives

In this section of two stories I will again present composite narratives of two people, this time both women. Each narrative is made up of pieces of experience of a number of individuals I know well. The names and identities of the individuals are not revealed for the sake of privacy. However the essential experiences described for each character are very real and not uncommon. The first person, whom I shall call Eriko, was born and brought up in America, but with a strong Japanese background. She aimed for full bi-culturality and succeeded. The second, Yukiko, initially lived in Japan but moved to other countries eventually settling in America. She initially sought full bi-culturality and succeeded at one point. However, important changes in her life caused her to recede a bit to a point where she is no longer Bi-Cultural.

Eriko's Story

Eriko was born in New York City. Her father was an expatriate Japanese businessman who was sent to America by his company before Eriko was born, then decided to stay here permanently. He left his former employer and struck out on his own. After a time and with hard work and well honed English language skills he became a successful businessman.

He took out American citizenship. He felt comfortable in America. Eriko's mother, however, was having a different type of American experience. While enjoying a more physically comfortable life than she had in Japan nevertheless she missed living there. She never felt comfortable in America and, not making much of an attempt to raise her ability to speak English, it stayed at a lower level. She maintained a Japanese atmosphere at home, including language, meals, following of cultural traditions and holiday celebrations and the display of artwork in her home. She tried to stress the use of Japanese language communications media, but of course most available radio and television programming was in English. While the fundamentally different orientations of her two parents—her father identifying more with America and her mother more with Japan—could have become a problem they worked hard to avoid open conflict about it. Her father acquiesced to the continuing (mostly) Japanese theme of his in-home scenario but lived the lifestyle many associate with middle-class American businessmen outside the home.

When Eriko was 4 years old and starting nursery school in New York her ability to speak English was found to be deficient and she had to take lessons in English as a Second Language. As she progressed through elementary school her English strengthened. She began answering in English questions posed by her father in Japanese. She always talked only Japanese with her mother. By the time she reached high school she was fully bi-lingual and had a circle of friends from both cultures, including some girls who overlapped, having also grown up with a mixture of the two cultures.

Eriko attended private English language school during the week and private Japanese language school on Sundays. She was a good student in both systems. Her main extra-curricular activity was dancing. She began with ballet as a small child and progressed through other dance genres as she grew older, particularly enjoying non-traditional dance forms. Privately her mother was troubled by Eriko's continuing drift away from a strictly Japanese lifestyle but understood that there was little she could do about it at that time. Occasionally the family visited relatives in Japan for short intervals. But Eriko's mother always felt that the visits were not enough. From time to time, mother and daughter would enter into dialogue about this particular subject. Initially Eriko resisted the idea that she could do more to raise the level of the Japanese part of her life experience. But eventually her attitude changed. By the time she graduated from the American college she had chosen to go to she was ready to look at additional avenues of personal growth.

Around that time many prominent American banks and financial service companies were opening up offices in Japan. They were eager to recruit young people who could speak both languages and understand both cultures—for initial training in the US, followed by an entry level but permanent job in Japan. Eriko's decision to sign up was welcomed by her mother, although outwardly she expressed regret that Eriko was going far away. Her father expressed genuine regret at Eriko's leaving but was resigned to accept whatever resulted from this decision. When Eriko got to Japan there were, of course, many colleagues in her workplace who had grown up in Japan. But there were also some young Americans. One of these was Michael, an American Caucasian security analyst whose father had been a US Naval officer and who had lived in various places around the world, including Japan once before. Eriko and Michael began dating. He introduced her to Japanese dance forms, which she studied and added to her reperatoire. After a time they were married and moved back to America to raise a family, settling in New Jersey. Eriko decided to concentrate on dance as a career and secured employment as a dance therapist in a rehabilitation center—work she finds fulfilling and consistent with her extra-curricular background.

Eriko's mother was satisfied that Eriko had experienced a significant period of living in Japan. Eriko's father was particularly glad to have her back and was thankful to her Gaijin (non-Japanese) husband for having precipitated this result.

Eriko had the benefit of growing up in America and experiencing the two cultures one way or another from the beginning. Her mother kept her anchored in Japan while her father did the same for America. She could from an early age speak both languages perfectly. She enjoys life with both her Japanese and American friends. And she is tuned in to nuances on both sides. Eriko earns an ACES 12—she is fully Bi-Cultural.

Yukiko's Story

The last story in this group which I will tell involves a composite woman I will call Yukiko. She was brought up in a small agricultural town in Western Japan. The Second World War had ended only a few years before and the American military still had a presence in the town. The soldiers were kind to the local Japanese children and provided a positive first exposure to America. While Yukiko's mother was a conservative woman, her father was very open to the changes then happening in Japanese society, including more knowledge of and influences from Western culture. At age twenty Yukiko asked for and received her father's permission to leave Japan temporarily, to spend two years going to college in England studying academic subjects plus improving her ability to speak English. During school holidays she travelled around most of Western Europe. At the end of the two year period she returned to Japan, intellectually greatly incremented by her experience in the West.

During her time away she had missed the distinctive culture of Japan. She missed her friends and family in Japan. Even though she corresponded with them regularly and occasionally spoke to them by telephone she knew they were far away. At the same time, she had developed a real affinity for the West and even after returning to Japan, maintained the desire to re-visit the West someday. She pursued those elements of a Western lifestyle that were available to a young Japanese woman, who was at the same time bound by strong Japanese societal traditions. She moved to Tokyo and went to work for the Japanese subsidiary of an American, Philadelphia headquartered multi-national company.

Yukiko's work environment was a culturally plural situation. There were a number of American expatriate executives in the company who spoke little if any Japanese. The working language that connected the far distant subsidiary with the parent company was English. All Japanese workers in positions where they would have interactions with the parent company were required to have at least a basic knowledge of English. Yet at the working level the Japanese spoke their native language among themselves. Some of the daily work rituals and office routines derived from America, some from Japan. As she was there longer the cultural duality of the situation had more and more appeal to Yukiko. She became more and more involved in those aspects of the company's operations that were conducted in English. She was often called on to translate written or verbal messages in one direction or the other. Years later, having saved some money, Yukiko decided she would take time off to finish her college education, begun earlier in England. She applied for and was admitted to The University of Pennsylvania, in Philadelphia.

She knew a few people in Philadelphia from her days with the multinational. One of these was Alex. She called Alex and they began seeing each other. As the relationship deepened over time Yukiko entered a period of intense relationship with the English language, building on the base she had acquired in Japan and England. She heard English all day on campus (there were probably other Japanese students or faculty members at the university but she didn't go out of her way to meet with them). Later each day she conversed only in English with Alex and his friends. She grew more and more interested in how America worked. She took courses in American History. She read book after book written in English, even outside of her required school work. After four years, on a beautiful Christmas Eve—snow softly falling and with spiritual music in the background—Yukiko and Alex were married in a 300 year old American country inn.

At that point Yukiko would have qualified as Fully Bi-Cultural. While still anchored in Japan she had made a strong effort to build up an American persona. While she didn't have much chance to interact with Japanese people, when those opportunities came she was able to move back and forth between the two cultures and languages easily. She was anchored in both cultures (A = 3). She was completely fluent in both languages (C = 3). She enjoyed leisure activities related to both cultures (E = 3) and, being from the beginning sensitive to the nuances of Japanese culture, she had reached a comparable level vis. a vis. American culture (S = 3). Attending social occasions involving Japanese people she became Japanese again. With Americans she mirrored American culture, with just a trace of Japanese and British speech accents betraying the fact that she hadn't lived in America her whole life.

The impending birth of their daughter Hiromi marked the beginning of another of Yukiko's transformations, this time in the direction of turning back to Japanese roots. She became firmly focused on ensuring that the part of Hiromi that was Japanese would not be overwhelmed by her American persona. Yukiko went to work for the American subsidiary of a Japanese company, ensuring that at least part of her daily work life would involve Japanese language communications and the understanding of Japanese culture even though she was living in America. She rose through the ranks to eventually become President. She spoke mostly Japanese at the office. After Hiromi was born Yukiko spoke to her almost exclusively in Japanese from the very beginning. She read Hiromi stories in Japanese. She enrolled Hiromi in a local Japanese language school that met on weekends. She went back to reading Japanese novels herself. She spoke frequently with family and old friends in Japan. Little by little she lost bits of the American cultural capability she had worked so hard to develop earlier. She was no longer able to relate to Americans as if she was uni-cultural in their culture.

Today my belief is that Yukiko is Bi-Cultural but not fully Bi-Cultural. Since her return to a strong Japanese orientation I feel that she has lost some of her American Anchoring (A) and has dropped to a 2 rating on that dimension—Fully anchored in Japanese culture but not American—and thus retreats from a full bi-culturality rating of 12.

The Game of Bi-culturalism

I set out in this chapter to examine the cultures of Hispanic and Asian immigrants to America through the prism of Phinney's quote reprised from the literature review in Chapter TWO and comprehending non-European immigrants developing bi-cultural identities (Phinney, op. cit., p. 78). I first reviewed scholarly writings of Korzenny and others bearing on the point and found them generally in accord with Phinney, at least with respect to Hispanics. Then I provided three narratives, constructed from conversations with Hispanic immigrants whose experiences in coming to and living in America were typical of many. The first two were selected based on their having different socio-economic starting points—one being from a wealthy family and one who had emerged from a situation where he and his family needed to start over in America, having left most of their belongings and wealth behind to emigrate here under emergency circumstances. I found that both had achieved the fully Bi-Cultural condition, with ACES ratings of 12 (highest attainable) and with the ability to now move easily between the two cultures (Hispanic and American) acting as if uni-cultural in each one. Then I reviewed the case of a third Hispanic who was not able to achieve full bi-culturality, finding Separation a more appropriate personal strategy. I examined similarities and differences and found—at least within this highly limited sample group—some elements of commonality and difference. In the successful Hispanic cases both had extensive early contact with American culture, emotional support from at least one person of importance to them for movement toward a bi-cultural adjustment strategy and success in using bi-culturality to play the game of life in America. The unsuccessful Hispanic did not display any of these factors.

Then I turned to Japanese respondents—as with the Hispanics, composites of people I knew intimately. I presented the case of one Japanese who I felt had achieved full bi-culturality. Among other topics the narrative covered her early background, containing elements of both Japanese and American cultures. Next I presented the story of a Japanese woman who showed another pattern—achieving full bi-culturality and then backing away from it in response to contextual changes that were important to her—providing at least some momentum for the idea that full bi-culturality, even if achieved, is not a permanent condition. This finding foreshadows the discussion in Chapter SEVEN to the effect that none of the conditions discussed in this book are necessarily permanent. Rather they are orientations that one can move into and out of according to changing and flexible individual adjustment needs and desires.

Of course these few interviews are not sufficient to do anything more than point to some possible directions for future study. However, it would seem that the observed trends were consistent with Phinney's assertion. From this initial limited look it would seem that there is nothing *inherent* in either the Hispanic or Japanese cultures that would prevent individuals from those cultures from achieving full bi-culturality. However, certain life patterns seem to affect ease of accomplishment. It might be more difficult for Japanese in that their original culture and language are more distant from what is expected in America, requiring a more energetic effort to build up an American persona. Additionally, for many Japanese, opportunities for intense early exposure to America and American culture might be less easily acquired than would be the case for Hispanics—stemming from geographical, contextual or other factors.

In the next Chapter I will review acculturational adjustment among Muslim immigrants.

Chapter FIVE

Hybrid Culture and the Muslims

Early in Chapter ONE I referred to the flexibility of acculturation study in the sense that the discipline in which the studier was working—e.g., sociology, psychology, anthropology, history etc.—played a big part in the characterization of acculturation phenomena in terms that were familiar in that discipline. I have tried to utilize many of these different frameworks as we have passed together through the initial American period of Uni-Culturalism (a society mainly made up of individuals from England or Northern Europe who shared a particularized culture), through The Melting Pot period where many from other parts of Europe chose an Assimilationist way of relating (although some withdrew into either what Berry would call Separation or the dual self-view of a Hyphenated Identity) and finally arriving at the bi-culturality often utilized by those who came more recently not from Europe at all but from Latin America and The Far East.

In this chapter I will take up another acculturative condition which has come to be referred to as *Hybrid Culturality*. Some say that Hybrid Culturality is just a different term for conditions we reviewed earlier, such as Hyphenated Identity or Bi-culturality. However for analytic purposes I will build a case for a separate construction of Hybrid Culturality, then go on to explore an important current minority group—American Muslims—in terms of the degree to which they fit this particular model. But before doing that I felt it might be helpful background to review how some prominent thinkers in the field have viewed The Cultural Hybrid.

Early Constructions of Cultural Hybridity

In 1993 Stuart Hall spoke of individuals who are "products of the cultures of hybridity." He goes on to say:

> These 'hybrids' retain strong links to and identifications with the traditions and places of their 'origin'. But they are without the illusion of any actual 'return' to the past. Either they will never, in any literal sense, return or the places to which they return will have been transformed out of all recognition by the remorseless processes of modern transformation. In that sense, there is no going 'home' again. (p. 361)

Tomlinson (1999) relates hybridization to *deterritorialization* which, for many, goes along with *globalization*. He says:

> . . . cultural mixing is unquestionably increasing with the advance of globalization . . . hybrid cultures may be a useful idea for grasping the sort of new cultural identifications that may be emerging . . . These complex transmutations of cultural practices and forms as they pass rapidly and effortlessly across national boundaries through the transnational cultural economy perhaps provide a figure for what a future 'globalized popular culture' may turn out to be like: different in character from the integrating, essentializing nature of national cultures, looser textured, more protean and relatively indifferent to the maintenance of sharp discrimination of cultural origin and belonging. (p. 147)

Rushdie (1991) refers to the "radically new types of human being" emerging from mass migrations . . .

> . . . people who have been obliged to define themselves—because they are so defined by others—by their otherness; people in whose deepest selves strange fusions occur, unprecedented unions between what they were and where they find themselves. (p. 124)

A characterization which, in my view, is particularly useful comes from Renato Rosaldo's *Foreward* to Garcia Canclini's book *Hybrid Cultures* (1995). Rosaldo writes:

> . . . Hybridity can be understood as the ongoing condition of all human cultures, which contain no zones of purity because they undergo

continuous processes of transculturation (two way borrowing and lending between cultures). (p. xv)

I believe that, looked at in this last way, it becomes easier to comprehend that, to a degree, cultural hybridity is intrinsically embedded in many other forms of adjustment, encompassing many different types of immigrants.

A New Construction of Cultural Hybridity

In my view it is helpful to think of the American pursuing *Hybrid Culturality* as developing in the form of a *pastiche of individually selected appropriated bits and pieces*, added onto a *basic ethnic, religious or other identity* that will probably remain as a strong chord in his/her personal symphony of personality development—although sometimes *affectively suppressed* in reaction to the perceived requirements of context. These are not individuals who want to change the world, or leave it or escape from their basic life orientation or construct internally an equal alternative.They simply want to build on what they consider a strong core with values and behaviours they find appropriate taken from people, situations, media and other things they are exposed to. Those developing in the mode of Hybrid Culturality appropriate some elements from the mainstream, mixing in some from their traditional culture, adding some from new sources that come onto their personal radar screens that are neither mainstream nor, for them, traditional. Hybrid Culturality contributes to America's development as a *cosmopolitan society* by making available a constant stream of eclectic individuals who can both borrow pieces of personality from others (as well as from characters in media and stories) and contribute some parts of their own personality. At the same time hybrid culture *benefits* from the *openness* of American society and its ability to provide comfort to those whose pastiche of individually determined personality elements does not follow any particularized set of *cultural imperatives*.

In pursuit of this idea let us explore other kinds of hybridity that we have come to see around us. Have you ever walked through a field of flowers, perhaps yellow ones, and noticed the occasional white flower— the same in all respects as the others except for the external colour? Or maybe you have visited a cornfield and found one plant out of thousands all around it that was producing ears of a different colour, size or texture? Chances are you were looking at *mutations*—results of natural differences in the gene structure of those particular individuals introduced randomly by nature. Some mutations comprehend *natural hybridity* which improves the organism's ability to do what it is supposed to do. Others do not improve it. Those that do are often reproduced artificially and harvested, the result sometimes being labeled a *hybrid strain*. Examples of this process could be cereal grains or lawn seed. One could say that the hybrid strain is different from the original mutation mainly in that human intervention has taken over to multiply individuals that had the desired characteristic built into them from the beginning.

Do you intend to look for a new car soon? Chances are you will at least consider what automobile companies are calling *hybrid cars*—cars that look basically the same as others but are capable of a fundamental change in their nature from being propelled by energy produced by gas to energy produced by electricity. Here the innovation—again affecting fundamental characteristics that dwell deep inside—rather than being produced by nature, was entirely produced by man *in response* to nature and the surrounding environment, specifically reacting to high gasoline prices and rising concern about auto pollutants. Then mass production followed on the man-made innovation.

The Cultural Hybridity I am discussing in this chapter incorporates both a fundamental deep down nature not born into the individual but developed early in life and added to in response to surrounding environmental and cultural forces later. In this case however the result remains an individual matter—resisting mass uniformity even if social forces attempt to impose it. The freedom immigrants find in America ensures individual adjustment opportunity for all, while presenting an environment lacking many rules some individuals are used to, causing discomfort to some.

For purposes of my argument I am selecting *American Muslim immigrants* as the model for discussion of *Hybrid Culturality*. Many Muslim immigrants have a strong, trans-national identity based on the faith of Islam which extends across many diverse ethnic or country of origin groups. This identity is at least partially based on the ideas of *divine authorship* of their scripture, its *exact maintenance* as it was given to them fourteen centuries ago, the *avowed completeness* of Islam as a religious system and its extension into detailed *rules of behavior*, variously articulated, that transcend what many would understand as expected correlates of particular religions. On the other hand, *individual adjustment patterns* are encouraged by the very *diversity of original ethnicities* of American Muslims—presenting, for many, ranges of exposures to new behaviours unheard of (or unthinkable) in their respective original cultures—combined with the openness of America and its tolerance for individually tailored solutions. American Muslims must operate in a context where there is no strong centralized Muslim religious or administrative infra-structure to stress uniformity, nor does this pressure come from American society itself as was the case for many in their original settings. Additionally, Muslim immigrants must deal with the constant condition of many mainstream Americans having little real knowledge of Islam and sometimes orienting toward them in terms of inaccurate, often negative stereotypes.

Many Muslims seek an individualized answer in America—selecting and blending together partial solutions that relate to parts of their overall condition in ways that seem individually appropriate. To better understand this relationship it is productive to examine the origins and early international growth of Islam, then to consider Islam in America, the latter mainly through the lens of Hybrid Culturality—the *blending of cultures* that has affected many—and finally to discuss *perceptions of terrorism* and other issues that define some parts of current Muslim context in America and serve to drive some toward more openly mainstream behaviours while increasing salience for others of traditional Muslim practice.

The Prophet Muhammed and the Early Development of Islam

While some Islamic scholars trace the roots of Islam back to the Biblical figures of Adam and Eve and others regard Abraham's son Ishmael as the father of the religion, most accept that the modern era of Islam began with The Prophet Muhammad. Muhammad was born to a family of exalted lineage whose fortunes had declined, leaving them poor, in the city of Mecca in what is now Saudi Arabia in 570 AD. Mecca at that time was a thriving commercial hub and center of the then current idol-based pagan religion. It was also a society sharply divided along tribal lines. While still a child Muhammad's parents died, leaving him to be raised by an uncle, Abu Talib.

Muhammad proved to be a thoughtful man and also a good businessman. At age 25 he was commissioned by a wealthy woman named Khadija, many years his senior, to take a camel caravan of her merchandise to Syria. Based on his superior performance Khadija approached him with a proposal of marriage, which Muhammad accepted making Khadija the first of his four wives. At that point Muhammad was no longer poor.

But Muhammad began to feel disenchanted with Meccan society, observing that with commercial riches had come a reduction in caring for the predicaments of the poor. Muhammad would wander off into the countryside to meditate. One day, at age forty, he underwent a transformational experience while meditating in a cave. The cave filled with an intense sense of presence, but no human being was visible. This was, according to Islamic tradition, The Angel Gabriel, sent from Allah to reveal the essential Holy Scripture of Islam *The Qur'aan.* This was the first of many visitations that would occur until Mohammad's death twenty-two years later.

Shaken by the experience, Muhammad consulted Khadija and together they visited some clergy from other religions. They told Muhammad that the experience of mortal people receiving divine Word was not unique and that he should be prepared to accept the responsibility of being The Prophet of Islam. Muhammad continued to have these divine revelations. Each time he would reportedly go into a trance-like state where he was receiving the Word directly into his being. As he was illiterate throughout his life, Muhammad would upon awakening dictate the Word he had been given to scribes who would write it down. The Word was given to Muhammad in Arabic and reportedly survives to this day with no change from what the scribes had written fourteen centuries ago—establishing a heritage tradition that is important for many Muslims.

Muhammad began on the task of converting the people of his home town of Mecca. However this activity was ill received by members of his and other clans, who had a vested interest in maintaining Meccan society as it was. When various offered inducements failed to stop Muhammad from preaching his monotheistic religion his enemies set up an embargo on the family business. A precipitous financial decline ensued, during which Khadija and Abu Talib died.

Just as things seemed hopeless, according to Islamic tradition The Angel Gabriel once again visited Muhammad and took him to Jerusalem where he reportedly ascended to Heaven from the site that is, in the present day, known as al-Aksa Mosque (or alternatively The Dome of the Rock). During his time in Heaven, Muhammad was given by Allah a comprehensive set of guidelines for living a good Muslim life and when he returned they were written into *The Qur'aan*. Some of these rules form part of the present day *Shari'a* (comprehensive rules for Muslim behaviour).

Eventually his Meccan enemies conspired to kill Muhammad but he escaped to Yathrib (the site of the present day Medina), where he was welcomed. Yathrib was, at that time, mostly a community of Jews but with some Muslim inhabitants. Historically wracked by feuding between the Muslims and the Jews and among the various Muslim tribes Yathrib came into a peaceful period as Muhammed rose to local power and showed his growing mastery of diplomacy. Eventually differences with the Jews developed (for example, they viewed a self-proclaimed non-Jewish Prophet with suspicion) and Muhammed expelled them from Medina. Muhammed's ability as a soldier and field general developed further as he built and led an army back to conquer first Mecca and then other places in what is now Saudi Arabia. Ultimately, in control of about 100,000 people spread over a substantial geographic area and with many options for governing style he chose to allow pre-existing locally oriented social and governmental systems to continue in force while personally operating through alliances. This approach became important as Islam spread to other areas—the pattern comprising first conquering resistance by force in the name of Allah but subsequently allowing local tradition to prevail in day-to-day secular and religious practice matters. While many in conquered lands embraced Islam, usually no requirement to do so was imposed. Muhammed died in 632 AD. At that time *The Qur'aan* as we know it today had been revealed, to be joined as Muslim Scripture by a book containing the teachings of Muhammed and referred to as *The Hadith* (See Footnote 5.1).

Islam spread rapidly after the death of Muhammed. Subsequent leaders moved against the Byzantine and Persian Empires. By the beginning of the fourteenth century The Ottoman Empire had formed, uniting vast areas under the banner of Islam.

The Ottoman Empire . . . also known in the West as the Turkish Empire, existed from AD 1299 to AD 1922. At the height of its power, in the 16th and 17th centuries, the tri-continental Ottoman Empire controlled much of Southeastern Europe, the Middle East and North Africa, stretching from the Strait of Gibraltar . . . in the west to the Caspian Sea and the Persian Gulf in the east, from the edge of Austria and Slovakia in the hinterland beyond Ukraine in the north to Sudan and Yemen in the south. The empire was at the center of interactions between Eastern and Western worlds for six centuries. (See footnote 5.2)

Following the example of Muhammed himself, the Ottomans constructed the governing of their territories as an *administrative* rather than a *religious* challenge. While Islam emerged as the dominant religion of The Ottoman Empire there were great differences between one region and another concerning religious practice and what it really meant to be a Muslim. These differences were tolerated—some believe even encouraged—by the Ottoman leadership.

In World War I The Ottomans chose the side that eventually lost and forfeited their vast land holdings—which became thirty-nine different countries, many of which exist with their original boundaries today and with their widely varied traditional cultures, treated with respect by The Ottomans, still largely intact. This point is important today because, unlike Europe where particular countries' Muslim immigrants tended to come from relatively few origin countries—usually with some pre-established colonial or other connection—the immigrant stream to America drew from original countries and cultures spread throughout the former Ottoman Empire and from other places. When this culturally heterogeneous Muslim group reached America many individuals found themselves interacting with other Muslims who were quite dissimilar to themselves.

Muslims in America

In the international sphere Islam has a very large presence—about 1.2 billion individuals worldwide, a total roughly equal to the entire population of The People's Republic of China. In the United States recent estimates of Muslim population have stretched from a low of 1.1 million to a high of 7 million—government information restrictions making a tighter definition difficult in the Muslim case. It is clear that American Muslims are a small percentage of the worldwide Muslim total, but with possibly an importance out of proportion to their small numbers in that they live in a country where they are free to experiment openly with cultural revisions if desired.

American Muslims come from diverse original ethnic backgrounds. Afridi (2001, p. 1) offers this comment:

Muslims in the United States reflect the diversity of the Islamic world and the diversity that is America. American Muslims represent a rich mosaic of ethnic, racial, linguistic, tribal and national identities that stretch from the Middle East to South Asia to Africa and beyond. The community (in America) includes immigrants with roots in more than 50 nations across the globe.

The original Muslims on American soil were slaves from West Africa brought over mostly in the eighteenth century. They brought their religion—acquired during Ottoman Times—with them. However, as this cohort became more and more displaced their original culture, including religion, was largely abandoned. In the nineteenth century other Islamic immigrants began to seek citizenship in the United States. Haddad and Lummus (1987) provide a brief history of this early Islamic development in America:

> (These) immigrants . . . were young men from rural areas who were often illiterate and with little knowledge of English. . . . Concerned with economic survival in a new land, they attempted to maintain a low profile and not draw attention to themselves or their religion. For the most part they had little Islamic consciousness or even knowledge of the fundamentals of the faith. Not having attended the mosque regularly at home they did not look to do so in the new land. . . . Often little integrated into American society, they had to bring young women from overseas to be their wives. (p. 156)

Looking at more recent times (twentieth century) Haddad and Lummus continue:

> . . . different (later) waves of immigrants have brought to America ideas and expectations of what it means to be Muslim. They came representing the concensus of what their fellow Muslims thought Islam should be at any given time. In the 1950s, nationalist Muslims emigrating to America brought a rational interpretation of Islam in which the particulars of Islamic observance such as regular prayer and attendance at the mosque are less important than living an ethically responsible life. At the same time, a few imams came holding up the ideals of specific Islamic practice with a stress on law and ritual. (p. 156)

After the US immigration laws changed in the mid 1960s (See Chapter ONE) it became easier for Muslims to emigrate to America. During that period large numbers came from many diverse original countries. For example:

- Arabs from the Middle East brought a more orthodox version of Islam with them.
- Muslim Iranians fled political chaos in the Khomeini Era. While Muslim they came from a Persian culture.
- Turks came from a culture that was, from the beginning, secular by design.
- Muslims from South Asia embodied a number of traditions. Following independence from England in 1947 many brought a strong post-colonial viewpoint. But there were differences. Indian Muslims came from years of living successfully, in relative harmony, side by side with a seemingly exotic, polytheistic Hindu culture. Pakistanis and Bangladeshis, on the other hand, emerged from a recent history of splitting from each other, each to pursue their own destiny.
- Many Palestinians and Lebanese came as wartime refugees.
- Muslims from West Africa came fleeing political upheaval and to pursue a better life.

After 9/11 the pendulum swung the other way and it became much more difficult for Muslims to emigrate to America. Nevertheless, as we have seen with Hispanics, the seeds of further growth in the American Muslim aggregate were already here. The birthrate among Muslim immigrants was significantly higher than in the American mainstream (Leonard, 2003, p. 4). Another source of growth in the overall American Muslim community came from (primarily) African-American converts to Islam. Today a substantial portion (sometimes estimated as high as 30 to 40%) of American Muslims comprise African-Americans who converted to Islam and their descendants (Leonard ibid, p. 4). Though not immigrants, nevertheless African-American converts contributed a unique sociological background and perspective to the overall American Muslim community. Here is a brief thumbnail history of African-American Islam, taken from Cateura (2005):

Islam returned as a significant aspect of African-American identity in the early period of the twentieth century. The movement was traced to the mysterious W. D. Fard, who appeared in Detroit. He trained Elijah

Poole to be his disciple, bestowing the name Elijah Muhammad. For a period of almost fifty years, Elijah Muhammed led what was known as The Nation of Islam. Many immigrant Muslims have retrospectively objected to the association of the term Islam with this movement as they have perhaps correctly pointed out that The Nation of Islam had little in common with the global practices and teachings of Muslims. . . . Indeed the racial (black supremacist) teachings of Elijah Muhammad . . . can best be seen as a mirror of the racist (in the other direction) Christian teachings of the late nineteenth/early twentieth centuries. The active leadership of the movement passed to Malcolm X, who attempted to radically turn the movement in the direction of orthodox Muslim belief. Malcom X was assassinated and the transition was completed by Elijah Muhammad's son Warith Dean Muhammad. (p. 13)

Today most African-American Muslims follow the orthodox (majority) Sunni tradition.

American Muslims' Fundamental Cultural Identity

Many Muslims have had to formulate a life in America that takes into account a strong religion originally developed in ancient times but with an ambiguous relevance today—argued variously as completely relevant by some, less relevant by others, necessarily more all-consuming by some, less by others. With this condition as background, additionally many Muslims now live in a country that is culturally far different from their original country, less understanding of the Islamic religion (in fact often misunderstanding it) and among other Muslims who are, in many cases, quite different from themselves. What patterns of adjustment are sought out? Haddad and Lummis relate to the point as follows (1987, p. 166):

> . . . it is . . . important for Muslims in America to view Islam as an overarching identity, linked with and yet finally independent of ethnic and national associations, a common bond holding together those of different backgrounds and customs.

Haddad and Lummis' above quoted view of *Ummah* (worldwide community of Muslim believers) membership being fundamental to American Muslim identity formation is by no means universal. An example of a dissenting view comes from Leonard, who in *Muslims in the United States* (2003) wrote as follows:

> . . . secular (American) Muslims do take pride in the high achievements of Islamic civilizations but do not identify themselves primarily through their religious heritage. (p. 46)

While I respect Leonard's position I believe that it is at most applicable to a small proportion of Muslims. Data I will present later in this chapter will tend to support what I believe is the majority view—that being part of the world-wide Ummah is an important and fundamental value for many Muslim immigrants.

The Sorbonne's Jocalyn Cesari provides helpful additional perspective (2004):

> The emergence of a 'New Muslim' minority, whose membership is rapidly growing, has been an unexpected consequence of Muslim settlement in the West. Its novelty resides in its *separation of religion from ethnicity* (italics mine). New Muslims have anchored their identity primarily within the transnational concept of *umma* (the timeless community of believers) rather than in national culture . . .
>
> . . . Muslims within the West generally base their religious identities upon one of two foundations: either a secularized bond with Islam that relativizes its demands or a fundamentalist attitude that demands respect for Islamic tradition in its totality, minutiae included. (p. 85)

Cesari's concept raises the (ethnically diverse) Muslim Ummah in affiliative importance over the individual immigrant's original ethnic identity (e.g., Pakistani, Iraqi) and, by implication, possibly over American self-definition as well. Cesari also establishes a conceptual division between a more *conservative*, traditionally bounded Muslim immigrant group and a more open, less bounded *liberal* group. Those who choose the conservative path would be more closely tied to the historic, detailed day-to-day living imperatives of the Islamic religion. Those who choose the liberal path are free to build on their fundamental Muslim structure by appropriating any of the broad range of non-Muslim behaviours and ideas available in America as part of a pastiche formation, or indeed to borrow alternate definitions of Islam from Muslims with different, (e.g., more liberal) origins and/or to mix in those parts of their original ethnic culture that they wish to maintain. This allows *multiple new forms of Muslim identity* to evolve and change on a constant basis.

Here are the words of Hassan, a liberal Pakistani Muslim living in America (2000):

> It is an exciting time to be an American Muslim. We stand at the threshold of redefining a centuries-old religion and carrying on Muslims' legacy of achievement. American freedom of thought, and separation from cultural amplifications of religious practice, are allowing American Muslims to adopt a leaner, more accurate Islam. This Qur'anic Islam is very compatible with Western lifestyle, as the vestiges of non-Western culture are dropped. (p. 176)

In my view, America is one of the few places where Hassan's "leaner" Islam, more "compatible with Western lifestyle" could develop today—at least among liberal Muslims like herself. For this reason, America's population of Muslims—relatively small in numbers compared to the world-wide presence of Islamic believers—may have disproportionate importance.

Muslim Identity Through a Research Lens

The American Muslim immigrant segment has not experienced the relatively large amount of empirical identity or lifestyle research that we saw earlier in the Hispanic case. Recently however a study of Muslims that was in my view well designed and executed by a reputable research company became available. This study (Pew Research Center, 2007) featured phone interviews with 1,732 Muslim individuals, of whom 65% were immigrants and 20% were African-American converts. Male/female split for the entire sample was fairly even at 54%/46%. In many cases sub-sample data were available for examination based on immigrant vs. convert respondent status, age and gender—thus allowing for selected more detailed looks inside the Muslim community. In some cases results were compared to parametric results for the entire country (sampled Muslims were roughly comparable to US totals in most demographic respects but slightly lower in age, income and education—not surprising for a mostly immigrant grouping). For immigrants, reasons for emigrating were divided, about half being pursuit of educational or economic opportunity, one quarter family issues and one fifth to escape conflict or avoid persecution. I reviewed the study particularly from the viewpoint of whether it did or did not support the idea of a basic split between those who could fit Cesari's descriptions of Muslim *conservatives vs. liberals* and whether there were judgmentally important *sub-group trends*. In doing this I focused particularly on four questions from the study which I felt were more relevant to my thesis. Questions, responses and brief discussions are presented below.

Table 5.1: Cultural Maintenance

Muslim immigrants should:	**Total sample**	**Immigrants**
Adopt American customs	43%	47%
Remain distinct	26%	21%
Both	16%	18%
Neither	6%	5%

Data showed only about one-fifth to one-quarter of the total favoured remaining more or less completely distinct as Muslims—the lower figure for immigrants. Most of the remainder favoured at least some degree of openness to mainstream customs. Men's responses were about the same as those of women. However deviations occurred when controlled by age (39% of 18-29 year olds wishing to remain distinct trended down to only 17% for those 55+). Additionally, African-American converts also scored high on this dimension (39% wishing to remain distinct).

Table 5.2: Construction of *Qur'aan*

Believe *Qur'aan*:	
Was written by Allah	86%
Was written by men	5%
Should be taken literally	50%
Is open to interpretation	25%

Nine out of ten respondents indicated Islam was important to them and nearly all of these (the 86% above) accepted that *The Qur'aan* contained the words of God. However, fully half as many said that the words in *The Qur'aan* could be interpreted in light of modern context as said that it should be literally followed. This result seems to me to show at least some sub-group acceptance of introducing individually relevant factors when constructing meaning from *The Qur'aan*.

Table 5.3: Self-definition

Think of yourself as:

Muslim first	47%
American first	28%

The same two sub-trends appeared as we saw earlier with respect to cultural maintenance. First there was again an age skew that indicated more religious investment on the part of younger people (Muslim first: age 18-29: 60%; older categories: trending down from 43% to 39%). Additionally African-American converts scored 58% on Muslim first identity). These trends could possibly be interpreted as responses to discrimination—experienced more frequently by young people (age 18-29: 42%) and African-American converts (46%) compared to the overall Muslim sample (33%). To provide a *rough external benchmark*, Pew (ibid) quotes another study they administered (Pew 2007A) among US Christians finding that 42% thought of themselves as Christian first, 48% American first. To the degree the studies were comparable these results could possibly suggest that young Muslims and African-American Muslim converts feel more strongly about the primacy of Ummah membership than older, primarily immigrant Muslim groups whereas the latter more closely approach overall patterns in American Christian faith taken as a whole—in some cases possibly due to older and maybe less discriminated against Muslims having absorbed at least some mainstream values.

Table 5.4: Adherence to Prayer Requirement

Frequency of prayer:

Five times per day	41%
One to five times per day	20%
Less or never	39%

Praying five times per day is one of the most fundamental and important requirements of Islam. Prayers do not always have to be said in a mosque. Roughly four in ten report following the requirement exactly. There appears to be a less observant middle group that complies but at a lower commitment level. Then there is a substantial percentage that fall well below the requirement. This could be suggestive of both a basic conservative vs. liberal split and a possible more blended group in the middle. I believe these above reported results are directionally support-ive of Ciseri's conservative vs. liberal dichotomy.

An earlier, less comprehensive quantitative study (Zogby 2004) showed some results that were similar to Pew (2007) above and some that differed slightly. Looking further back, a largely qualitative study of Muslims by Haddad and Lummus (1987), authors quoted on conceptual points earlier in this chapter, found in their interviews an array of "worldviews" which included the following three: *Liberals*—These were the least religious, (often incorporating influences from outside Islam into their American lifestyle—material in parens mine). *Conservative but Westernized*—These adhered to the minimum Islamic requirements deal-ing with personal piety, dietary restrictions and prescribed practices. *Evangelicals*—These emphasized scripture and emulating the life of The Prophet Muhammad. They (took) special care to fulfill *all* the minute prescriptions and proscriptions of Islam. They tended to be isolationist and centered in a small group of like minded Muslims (p. 170). These results again directionally support the presence of a group of American Muslim immigrants dedicated to following the imperatives of the reli-gion exactly and other groups which take a less literal viewpoint, appar-ently blending a basic Muslim identity with customs appropriated from other domains of life in America.

Drivers of Muslim Cultural Hybridity

While American freedom and openness to individual choice have pro-vided a *welcoming environment* for those Muslims and others who have opted to pursue an adjustment strategy of Cultural Hybridity there are also factors that advance the *need for at least consideration* of this kind of individually based blended strategy among those who have not yet decided how to form their life patterns in America. In this section I will, *for illustrative purposes,* discuss a few of these factors—particularly as they apply to Muslims. I believe that some similar factors could be found in other immigrant cultures, particularly those such as Indian Hinduism that feature concepts, practices and ideologies that are far from the Ameri-can mainstream—equating to potential attraction of Cultural Hybridity to a wider range of immigrants.

Perceptions of Terrorism

I believe that fundamentalist terrorism, whether on American soil or elsewhere, affects the majority of peace-loving American Muslims in several ways, foregrounding for some the possible appropriation of be-havior patterns likely to be seen by the mainstream as less Muslim and more mainstream (more liberal). Others wish to continue to be viewed as more commited to the moral compass built from basic Muslim values, specifically excepting terrorism. Some Muslims are concerned that nega-tive stereotypes of them which exist among the mainstream make it harder for them to adopt aspirational American lifestyles. Some Muslims are concerned that extreme interpretations of Islamic requirements, used by some to justify terrorist acts, are contrary to the intent of those who shaped Islam in ancient days.

Historically, mainstream America has not known very much about Muslims or about the Islamic religion. Particularly in the Post 9/11 era this vacuum has often been filled by a negative stereotype. As Cateura explains (2005):

> Much of the confusion and fear that Americans are experiencing may arise in part from the fact that many in this country know nothing about the vast majority of its American Muslim people, who do *not* comprise a like-minded mass of white-robed fundamentalists, as they do in some North African and Middle Eastern countries, but who are individuals in mostly Western dress, with diverse personal opinions, beliefs and accomplishments.They are our doctors, police, teachers, grocery and restaurant owners, bureaucrats, taxicab drivers, construc-tion workers, small business owners, travel agents. (p. 265)

A new Pew Research Center project (2006) reported polling over 3,000 *American mainstream* adults and finding that 58% responded that they knew "Not very much" or "Nothing" about Muslims. Asked to sum-up impressions of Muslims, respondents were twice as likely to select negative descriptors (e.g., "fanatic, radical, terrorists") as posi-tive ones (e.g., "devout, peaceful, dedicated"). 70% constructed the Muslim religion as being "very different" from their own.

Returning to the Pew (2007) poll of *Muslim* respondents discussed earlier in this Chapter, many (76%) also felt strong concern about Mus-lim fundamentalist extremism. Only 5% had a favourable view of Al-Qaeda. Both the mainstream American public and the Muslim minority tend strongly to reject terrorism. However, many in the mainstream American group seem often not to distinguish between the small number of Muslim individuals who are actually involved in planning or carrying out terrorist activities in America and the vast majority of American Muslims who simply want to pursue a peaceful life. As mentioned earlier about one third of Muslims reported having experienced some discrimination in America. Over half (53%) believe the environment for Muslims in America has gotten worse since 9/11.

I believe that this context of lack of understanding of their minority culture by mainstream America, suspicion and sometimes actual discrimination against them could lead to different types of Muslim responses. Some could move toward the mainstream by, for example, dressing and acting in such a way as to minimize the perception or characterization of them as Muslims—i.e., to effect individual adjustment by appropriating elements of the mainstream culture. Others could purposely try to avoid contact with the mainstream. Some could move in the opposite direction, seeking solace through even closer association with conservative Islam.

As alarming for some Muslims as the prejudice and discrimination directed toward them by the mainstream is what they believe to be misuse of traditional Muslim concepts in the interests of advancing Islamic fundamentalism in the present day or, even worse, the complete disregarding of these concepts—of ancient origin and believed by many to be still valid. Muslims need to find a way to rationalize these conflicts, an individualized way of constructing reality that makes sense and allows them to go forward with their lives in America.

In the publication *What Does Islam Say About Terrorism?* Momin (2006) states:

> Islam considers all life forms as sacred. However the sanctity of human life is accorded a special place. The first and foremost right of a human being is the right to live." He goes on to quote *The Qur'aan* 6:151 ". . . take not life, which God hath made sacred, except by way of justice and law . . ."

> Even in a state of war, Islam enjoins that one deals with the enemy nobly on the battlefield. Islam has drawn a clear line of distinction between the combatants and the non-combatants of the enemy country. As far as the non-combatant population is concerned such as women, children, the old and the infirm etc. the instructions of the Prophet Muhammed (Peace Be Upon Him) are as follows: Do not kill any old

person, any child or any woman. Do not kill monks in monasteries. Do not kill the people who are sitting in places of worship. (p. 3)

Indiscriminate mass bombings carried out in recent years, both in America and elsewhere, could seem to many Muslims inconsistent with these ideas. Abdalati provides classic Muslim concepts as follows (op. cit.):

> . . . life is a dear and cherishable asset and no sensible or normal person would like to lose it by choice. Life is given to man by God, and He is the only Rightful One to take it back; no one else has the right to destroy a life. This is why Islam forbids all kinds of suicide and self-destruction . . . (p. 28)

Yet suicide bombers claim hero status through what they believe is martyring themselves for a righteous cause—believing themselves to be on their way to Paradise.

Abdalati (ibid) presents this position:

> Everything we do in this world, every intention we have, every move we make, every thought we entertain, and every word we say are all counted and kept in accurate records. On the Day of Judgement they will be brought up. People with good records will be generously rewarded and warmly welcomed to the Heaven of God, and those with bad records will be punished and cast into Hell. (p. 13)

I believe that conflicts like these are not clearly understood by the American public, who take public statements of extremists as representing the views of many, if not all, Muslims. Additionally, many in the Muslim community understand the lack of mainstream comprehension. Some Muslims could react by attempting to appear more in the American mainstream by, for example, living among mainstream Americans rather than with many other Muslims close by, borrowing behaviours they see around them in the mainstream and moving further toward a pastiche hybrid personality combination.

Dealing with Apparent Inconsistencies Within Islam

Even though Islam stresses the importance of living in accord with *Shari'a* law which encompasses many aspects of both religious and secular life, often Muslims find ambiguities and inconsistencies with which they must deal if they are to have a meaningful life in America, where Muslims of many different backgrounds and traditions have come together. An example of this kind of issue is the wearing of the *hijab* or head covering by Muslim women. The original requirement, as stated in *The Qur'aan* does not comprehend head covering at all. Here is the passage (33:53):

> . . . and when you ask (the Prophet's ladies) for anything you want, ask them from before a screen: that makes for greater purity for your hearts and for theirs.

The transmogrification of this statement into a requirement for women to wear a head covering was an interpretive decision by an Islamic judge or scholar later in a particular time and place. There are Muslim countries today where the wearing of the hijab has become a legal imperative (e.g., most Arab countries). On the other hand, there are some countries where it is optional. In Turkey it is illegal to wear the hijab, at least at university. Consequently there could be a legitimate ambiguity as to what is the right course of action regarding wearing the hijab in America—with options open involving appropriation of alternate interpretations that might not have been present in the original country.

Some ambiguities come from *The Qur'aan,* for example relationships with Christians. All three of the major monotheistic religions surviving to this day are believed by Muslims to be descended from a common source: Abraham. This common origin is, according to Muslim tradition, to be taken seriously. And practitioners of any one of these religions are to be treated as "brothers" and "sisters" in the sense of worshiping the one God in their own way.

The Qur'aan, 3:84 states:

> . . . We believe in Allah, and in what has been revealed to us and what was revealed to Abraham, Isma'il, Isaac, Jacob, and the Tribes, and in (the Books) given to Moses, Jesus and the Prophets from their Lord: we make no distinction between one and another of them . . . (see Footnote 5.2)

On the other hand, in the following passage from *The Qur'aan* (as well as others) it is established that all Sins can be forgiven by Allah except acceptance of God(s) other than Him. 4:48 states:

Allah does not forgive that partners should be set up with Him; but he forgives anything else, to whom He pleases; to set up partners with Allah is to devise a sin most heinous indeed.

The Christian construction of Jesus as The Son of God thus sets up a dialogic conflict between Muslims and Christians which echoes in Islamic fundamentalist rhetoric even today. The basis for the conflict is that Muslims reject The Holy Trinity. Therefore they can look at Christians as violators of 4:48, cited above, and other similar passages they consider mandated to them directly from Allah. Muslim rejection of The Holy Trinity can add to the distrust of Muslims among Christians. The resolution of religious issues like this could lead to a compromise or blended solution as many Muslims might find some aspects of Christian culture attractive.

Imported Issues

Sometimes Muslim immigrants bring with them issues that were current and unresolved in their home countries. Such issues may not even be relevant in America. Alternatively, the immigrant individual may choose the solution that seems best to him in America and blend it into his overall personality mix. An example comes from present day Saudi Arabia. Conflicts between the Saudi version of Shari'a law and international culture impinging from outside are discussed in House's *Wall Street Journal* article (7 April 2007) entitled *For Saudi Women, A Whiff of Change:*

> The tug of war between tradition and modernity plays out in virtually every aspect of Saudi society, but nowhere more so than in the lives of its women. Unmarried men and women are forbidden to speak alone unless they are related. Yet the internet now makes it possible for them to exchange phone numbers—and then phone calls. Couples who dine out are segregated behind portable partitions to keep them from being seen by single men. Yet the sexes mix at the new Al Faisaliah shopping mall food court as they select from Dunkin' Donuts and McDonalds. Women are supposed to wear a long garment called an abaya when strangers are present, yet increasing numbers don it only outdoors and dress in Western clothes at the office. . . . The Saudi monarchy faces these and other social forces . . . that it constantly strives to balance to maintain its monopoly on political power. (p. A4)

Saudis who come to America can usually choose between wishing to maintain behaviours from their home culture or to appropriate adjustments from other Muslim cultures or perhaps to adopt a more American outlook. In America it tends to be an individual decision.

No Institutional Mechanism for Resolution

Dealing with the kinds of issues described above, where there are legitimate opposing positions possible, could be more impactful in America than in many Muslims' countries of origin, where there is a strong prevailing Muslim societal tradition favoring one viewpoint or another. In America the mainstream society usually does not stipulate "the answer" for Muslims and the lack of a central religious or administrative authority could become a more serious issue. Geliner discusses the conceptual rationale for the lack of Islamic infra-structure as follows (1981):

> Islam is the blueprint of a social order. It holds that a set of rules exists, eternal, divinely ordained, and independent of the will of men, which defines the proper ordering of society.This model is available in writing. It is equally and symmetrically available to all literate men, and to all those willing to heed literate men. These rules are to be implemented throughout social life.

> Thus there is in principle no call or justification for an internal separation of society into two parts, of which one would be closer to the deity than the other. Such a segregation would contradict both the symmetry or equality of access and the requirement of pervasive implementation of the rules. The rules of the faith are there for all, and not just or specially for a subclass of religious specialists—virtuosos. In principle, the Muslim, if endowed with pious learning, is self-sufficient or at any rate not dependent on other men, or consecrated specialists. . . *Thus, officially, Islam has no clergy and no church organization,* . . . (italics mine). (p. 1)

Some Muslim countries have panels of Islamic scholars to render interpretations of issues made ambiguous by the *technical* progress of their societies. Some have specially constituted religious courts, which operate independently of the civil court systems. America does not have these institutions. Accordingly, appropriateness of courses of action to be chosen in situations of ambiguity is often a matter of individual preference for American Muslim immigrants—an individual choice that is consistent with individually determined Hybrid Culturality.

Conversations with Muslims

To add another dimension to the theory and research about Muslims which I presented earlier I met and had substantive discussions with a wide range of followers of Islam—from students to college professors to writers and artists to imams (religious leaders) to everyday working people. Additionally I introduced variation as to country of origin so as to get a relatively broad array of viewpoints: Egypt, Saudi Arabia, Pakistan, India, Bangladesh, Lebanon and Palestine. I also talked with several people who had converted to Islam from other (Christian) relgions.

The most commonly expressed idea featured the primacy of the *Ummah* as a kind of personality development bedrock. In virtually every case Muslims believed that their religion came before their ethnicity, nationality, race or anything else around which a basic orientation could be formed. At the same time many stressed the wide variation in backgrounds of American Muslims and correspondingly wide variation in specific constructions of what it meant to be a Muslim. Many pointed out that America was very different from the places they originally came from—in that (despite some discriminative acts encountered from time to time) there was embedded in the social fabric of the American nation a certain tolerance for diversity that they were not used to, at least at the beginning of their time here. This made some feel insecure, that they were living in a kind of cultural diaspora or wasteland where strong "healthy" norms of behavior were missing. Many expressed the feeling that norms and attitudes pertaining inside the specific home in which a Muslim was raised played a very important role in how those same individuals would express their relationship with Islam after coming to America. Several people commented that America tended to move one to extremes—in that those who came here very devout tended to remain devout or become even more so, while those who did not closely follow the dictates of Islam prior to coming to America were even less likely to move in that direction here. An imam told me that while he knew that some Muslims did not follow the religious dictates strictly—engaging in behaviours such as drinking alcohol, allowing girls to date or not wear the *hijab* and not following prescribed prayer rituals still they were Muslims and needed to be treated as brothers and sisters whose specific relationship was with Allah. He did go on to say that when the Day of Judgement came for such individuals that the full array of their behaviours and actions on Earth would be examined.

In view of subtrends indicated in the Pew research presented earlier in this chapter I asked whether individuals were aware of heightened identification with the religion among African American converts or among younger Muslims. Regarding African Americans, some felt there was a cultural fault line that ran between immigrants and converts. Others enlarged on the point by arguing that the converts, being mostly African American, felt a stronger connection to Islam and knew more about it simply because of their previous cultural and ethnic struggles and the additional sensitivity this gave them. Regarding more piety by the young there were mixed opinions. Most felt that young Muslims tended to be more religious than their parents. Others stressed a desire on the part of these younger Muslims, particularly teenagers, to blend in with the mainstream.

Finally I asked many Muslims how the presence of terrorists and terrorism in the world affected them. Virtually all of those I talked with strongly condemned terrorism, often pointing out that terrorist acts were specifically forbidden by *The Qura'an*, not encouraged. Many pointed out that the concern that many mainstream Americans had about terrorism, coupled with what they perceived as a lack of much knowledge about Muslims, produced a climate that was not helpful. Many described acts of discrimination that had been perpetrated against them or those they knew because of their status as Muslims. Almost all wished that the environment would change to the point where they could fully enjoy the benefits America had to offer.

The American Laboratory for Muslim Cultural Experimentation

Approaches to governing constituent regions which began with Muhammed, featuring the allowance of *local culture, tradition and piety* to continue to prevail within an overall framework of Islam, were maintained through the great Ottoman Empire which ended with the close of World War I. At that point there were many countries and societies which followed Islam as a basic foundation but had built on that foundation in different ways. Some, such as Saudi Arabia, Pakistan and heavily Arab countries, had become closed, bounded societies where close adherence to Islamic imperatives was expected, and where in many cases the society formed its daily rhythms around the requirements of Islam to provide support. Others, such as Turkey and the Muslim countries of North Africa headed in a more secular direction, but again in a way that respected a national ethnicity. Not all people in any particular country reacted to their particular context in the same way. Some were more devout than others, depending more on the specific socialization practices in particular families than on the rules of their particular society— which had to be followed but not necessarily strongly believed in. Some individuals were more curious than others about what life was like in other places. The stream of Muslim immigrants to America contained a substantial *diversity of backgrounds*. When this complex, multi-faceted, heterogenous stream of people got to America many found that they were in a place very different from where they came from—a place where individuals could develop not necessarily along lines set down for them by their government or their society but in ways in which they as individuals found comfort. While some felt the right way for them was to continue closely following Islam, or to closely follow the lifeways of their ethnic country background many felt that a *blended* result was right for them. These embarked on what could be described as a great experiment in open individual development for Muslims, an experiment in Hybrid Culturality.

Outside of America such experiments have been rare in the Muslim world. In view of terrorist attacks by radical Islamic fundamentalists that we read about with unfortunately increasing frequency (along with almost universal condemnation of these attacks) it may be fair to ask whether Islam can afford not to see the American experiment as an attractive cultural alternative. Certainly American Muslims represent only a small proportion of the worldwide total of the followers of Islam. But can the results from this numerically tiny laboratory spread to other parts of the wider Muslim world? Will those of other countries that have a commitment to Islam and possibly also a strong sense of national identity come to America to live in a society where other themes can be blended in and adopt a similar Hybrid Culturality? These are important questions for the future.

Chapter SIX

Technology and Post Culture

In Chapter FOUR I compared Hispanic immigrants to Japanese immigrants with respect to whether it seemed more difficult for one group or the other to achieve and maintain the condition of *full bi-culturality*. I formed preliminary impressions that full bi-culturality could be a more difficult condition for Japanese immigrants even though there did not seem to be anything inherent in their culture to prevent it. There were certain life patterns that seemed to show up in the backgrounds of *individuals* who became fully bi-cultural, patterns that were not as consistent for those who were not able to achieve and maintain the condition suggesting the hypothesis of greater Japanese difficulty. An example of such a pattern would be intense early exposure to America—possibly not as easy for many Japanese to accomplish because of geographical or other factors.

In Chapter FIVE I showed how some American immigrants of Muslim background utilized a strategy of *Hybrid Culturality* to structure their adjustments to life in America. In their case Hybrid Culturality, which is neither universal to Muslims nor restricted to them, commenced with a *strong basic identity* (the feeling of belonging to the worldwide community of believers in the Islamic religion) and was further articulated by the *appropriation of different cultural elements* to which they were exposed resulting in a *cultural blend* whose exact makeup at any point in time varied at the level of the *individual person*. These different cultural elements reached them through, for example, exposure to co-religionists who had grown up with different interpretations of what it meant to be a Muslim, as well as other cultural influences.

In this Chapter I will discuss *Post Culturality*—an orientation which, like Hybrid Culturality, could pertain to potential or actual immigrants as well as more broadly to those who are not immigrants. In the *Post Cultural orientation* all semblance of bounded culture has disappeared. For purposes of this book I define a *post cultural person* as one who can *perceive and react to contextual and interpersonal changes fluidly—an orientation favoured by the various conditions that the person might have experienced.* A Post Cultural person constructs understandings of changes that make sense to him, allowing him to move in and out of various orientations, depending on what is favoured or seems appropriate at the time. I will put forward the idea that, like the Hispanic/Asian comparison above, it seems easier for some people to contemplate Post Culturality than for others. I will suggest that a deep understanding of and relationship with newly emerged *advanced information and media technologies* is helpful in such contemplation. However such understanding and relationship *do not seem absolutely critical*, as broader forces which introduce the potential for a *less bounded, more cosmopolitan outlook*—such as travel, schooling, friendships, leisure reading, artifacts and exposure over time to more traditional media such as radio, television, newspapers, magazines, motion pictures and other news and entertainment vehicles—can, for some, have a similar or supplementary effect.

In pursuing this argument I will start with a discussion of *the technologies of social saturation* as first described by Gergen in 1991. I will show how these have developed massively in a relatively short period of time. I will show that one of the key new technologies, the internet, has to date developed at different rates in different places around the world— a differential that is undergoing some correction in that the places "furthest behind" in terms of internet penetration are also seeing the fastest growth in internet presence. In my view, this trend could possibly foreshadow a day when increased international connectivity, instant and easy access to large amounts of information and exposure to new opinions and ways of life will be even more broadly available worldwide, independent of geographic location, political or social boundaries. This environment should allow a greater number of individuals to develop a *more cosmopolitan outlook* and accelerate the tendency even now observable for discrete, bounded cultures to recede as the characteristics of a post cultural era are more clearly and broadly articulated. I will once again look to the social scientific literature for insights to clarify the breakdown of conventional cultures in this environment.

Subsequently I will draw on my own experience and that of my teenage daughter Nicole to better focus the differences in developmental context between someone who is growing up with advanced technology today and one who grew up without it many years ago. This comparison will address the *helpfulness but non-essentiality* of advanced information technology in structuring Post Culturality as an end-state. Finally I will offer some hypotheses regarding factors that lead individuals toward or away from Post Culture. The next and final chapter will provide an overall review of the development of acculturation among American immigrants as a social process, along with some personal reflections.

The Technologies of Social Saturation

In 1991 Gergen predicted an information technology revolution. In writing about *the technologies of social saturation* in *The Saturated Self: dilemmas of identity in contemporary life* he said:

> These developments—computers, electronic mail, satellites, faxes—are only the beginning. Innovations now emerging will further accelerate the growth of social connectedness. At the outset is the digitization of all the major media—phonograph, photography, printing, telephone, radio, television. This means that the information conveyed by each source—pictures, music, voice—is becoming translatable to computer form. As a result, each medium becomes subject to the vast storage and rapid processing and transmission capabilities of the computer. Each becomes subject to home production and worldwide dissemination. We now face an age in which pressing a button will enable us to transmit self-images—in full color and sound—around the globe. (p. 60)

At the time these words were written advanced information and media technologies were just beginning to gain momentum. In 2006 Friedman observed:

> . . . at this point—the mid-1990s—the platform for the flattening of the world (phenomenon of enabling easy, quick and complete individual connectivity between and among individuals anywhere in the world) had started to emerge. . . . the falling walls (decline of Communism in Europe and consequent elimination of barriers to communication between millions of people), the opening of Windows, the digitization of

content, and the spreading of the Internet browser seamlessly connected people as never before. (p. 80)

Developing Friedman's point further I view the emergence of the internet over the last decade or so as an important key to major changes happening in the world of 2008. The internet delivers instant, easy access to vast amounts of information and provides a wide range of instant research, option definition and problem solving. It compresses time and space and has spawned applicational technologies which have increased local, national and international connectedness to an unprecedented degree.

The viral growth of *websites* could be interpreted as one marker of the internet's growing importance. Numbers recently published by Netcraft, a supplier of data to the information technology industry, showed that in 1991 (the year when Gergen wrote the words above) there were few, if any, websites as we know them today. As of May 2007 there were 118 million websites, situated on server computers all over the world but each accessible via computers in any other part of the world. Websites were being added to the world total at the rate of over 4 million per month (Netcraft, 2007, p. 1). While some of these sites are guarded by passwords and other devices that preclude entry into that specific site, nevertheless the amount of information that has become available seems to me impressive.

Search engines such as Google use advanced technology to respond almost instantly to inquiries requesting identification of the *addresses* of websites containing specific information. An entire industry (web search engine marketing) has developed based on commercial companies' desires to appear in an advantageous position when consumer searches for their kinds of products are initiated.

Many websites feature *internet chatrooms* and *bulletin boards*. In my view the importance of these resides in allowing the formation of relationships with people previously unknown (and, for all practical purposes, unknowable) all over the world, connected by similar interests. In fact, many utilize chatrooms to *play* at being someone else—a boy can "become" a girl, an old person can "become" young, an American can "become" British, a person anticipating a new life style interest can "try out" a new, different identity to determine comfort level in advance. Many websites have been developed involving games that can be played either individually or against other people who log on to the site at the same time, even if not known to the original player.

With internet connectivity came *derivative communication technologies* such as *e mail*—a much easier and quicker method of communication than written memos and much more cost-effective than use of the telephone in situations where voice communications are not a necessity. It is not necessary to know where a potential recipient is physically located to send him an e mail. E mails can be responded to or forwarded with just a few keystrokes. Millions upon millions of e mails are sent every day. Recently *e mail marketing* (sending out large numbers of specialized e mails aimed at selling products or services, sometimes personalized to the recipient, at relatively low cost and collectively called *spam*) has developed as a separate medium, spawning services known as *spam filters* for interception and to keep the incoming volume of e mails under control. *Links* embedded in e mail messages and websites allow instant transfer from one screen or site to another. *Instant messaging* has also grown, enabling subscribers to particular services to carry on a text dialogue on-line at virtually no incremental cost and usually independent of physical distance between participants. The internet has enabled a new medium called a *web log* or *blog*—a popular type of personal website often used to voice an originator's private opinions about topics of interest and allowing for input from visitors to the site. Anyone with access to the internet can initiate a blog. *Social networking sites* such as MySpace and Facebook have made it possible for millions of people, often young and looking for contacts with others, to expand their circle of those with whom they could have some relationship. In fact, these sites have generated some controversy as the openness with regard to personal detail can work against the interests of individual privacy. A further advance, presently centered in a site called YouTube, allows personally made videos to be sent over the internet and posted on a server. Often these videos are made with digital cameras, in lieu of still pictures, and sent through the computer over the internet in a process called *streaming*. Word of particularly important or otherwise noteworthy videos can spread quickly, building up a substantial audience through individuals logging on to the website and downloading the chosen video.

Even such previously staid institutions as the encyclopaedia have been transformed by the internet. *Wikipedia*, sometimes used as a source of information for this book, is such an *open document*—changeable at the discretion of the user and further providing the opportunity for people to connect across time and space. This is an example of a broader transition in media involving the *moving of control of content and access over to users*—a phenomenon I believe to be of great significance to consumer marketing companies, who had grown accustomed to a passive consumer with limited control over the content to which he was exposed. Rochelle Lazarus, the Chairperson of Ogilvy & Mather Worldwide, a major advertising and communications company, said in a recent speech: "The role consumers play has changed profoundly—they decide when, where and how they are going to consume entertainment." She added that while previous generations of advertisers worked as an intrusion, consumers can now "work around" them. "We have to be invited in," she said. "We have to entertain or provide information that is valuable. We have to do things well enough to surprise and delight our consumers so they want to engage with us" (reported by Lauren Bell in industry weekly *DMNews,* October 17, 2007).

The grand array of electronic advances and offerings faces an equally impressive array of *internet users*. The Miniwatts Marketing Group provides information on worldwide internet usage (see Footnote 6.1). Their figures show that—as of 2007—1.1 billion people worldwide had access to the internet—a rate of over 16%. While, as a subsequent section will show, there are still many places left in the world where internet penetration is currently negligible, on balance one person in six worldwide has at least theoretical access to the internet at this time.

An additional device for connectivity is the cellular (or mobile) telephone, of which there are about 2 billion presently extant (See Footnote 6.2). In a 26 March 2007 *Wall Street Journal* supplement entitled *What's New in Wireless* Sharma (2007) looks at likely future trends in the *expansion of functionality of the cellular phone*:

> In the next two to three years, consumers will be able to get TV broadcasts on their cellphones with better picture quality than current video offerings—and a greater range of live programming from major networks . . . Users will also get sophisticated software applications for surfing the mobile Web, and more services to connect with friends, share videos and exchange photos. And they'll likely see mobile devices that can roam seamlessly across Wi-Fi hotspots (places where wireless internet is available), cellular networks and new high speed data networks, bringing a much faster and smoother surfing experience. (p. 1)

In other domains, *Voice-Over-Internet Protocol (VoIP)* telephony has reduced the cost of international phone calls to just pennies per minute, allowing more frequent and longer phone conversations with friends and family far away. While this easy and low cost connection could tend to maintain anchoring to a more bounded culture (as when an immigrant calls home) yet it introduces new horizons of information and input for those on the other end of the call. Additionally, *satellite delivered television* has fundamentally changed the nature of ethnic diasporic experiences in many places. In America, for instance, it is now possible to receive live local news and entertainment programming via satellite from home country or some other possibly unfamiliar country in 22 different language/culture formats—from French, German and Italian to Farsi, Hebrew, Urdu and Vietnamese (See Footnote 6.3). *Cable television and associated technologies (e.g., VCR, TiVo)* have spread rapidly in industrialized countries, vastly increasing the range of viewing options—often up to levels of 500 or more simultaneous channel availabilities—and even eliminating the requirement to watch the programming in real time. News coverage has vastly improved. Now reporters from CNN and other specialized networks provide close-up, live coverage of major events happening around the world. It is often possible to watch contrasting coverage of the same far away event—and rather than accepting only the first reporter's construction of it, to allow for a fuller, more informed perspective on what is happening, its meaning and its importance. Even enemies can now easily communicate with each other. Television stations such as Al Jazeera supplement terrorist websites by serving as vehicles for communication and propaganda to the mainstream world as well as to terrorist followers.

In America and other advanced countries *internet cafes, libraries and other public access points and attractive equipment installment purchase or rental plans* allow even those of modest means access to the most up to date technology. It seems to me that one effect of these great advances in availability of technology, at least in America, has been to substantially raise the degree to which many people here are actually or potentially connected to others—being therefore in an improved position to acquire unusual knowledge, appropriate new behaviours and reduce reliance on traditional culture for the making of meaning. Those who choose to participate also have instant access to a huge variety of information, experiencing a speeded up form of reality characterized by time and space compression. I refer to this condition as *The Ether*-World—a world entered and exited at will via connection with modern media and information technologies and representing an *endogenous counterpart*—

an existential condition that comprises relationship with both technology and potentially with other people articulated in an electronic cosmos.

The next section will start to elaborate a worldwide picture by examining international internet penetration.

The International Presence of the Internet

This section will provide a closer look at the international spread of the internet, a key component of the technologies of social saturation. While there are other components, the internet carried with it many of the important *specific connectivity feature advances* enabled by the overall revolution in information technology. The Miniwatts Marketing Group, a supplier of information to the technology industry referred to previously, periodically publishes statistics on internet development worldwide on its website (see Footnote 6.1). The tables below present selected data arrays developed from their 2007 report. The tables show a wide discrepancy in current internet presence but also a situation that is rapidly changing.

Table 6.1: Continental Population and Internet Penetration

Region	% world pop'n	% country pop'n with i/n access
Africa	14.2%	3.6%
Middle East	2.9%	10.0%
Asia	56.5%	10.7%
S. America	8.5%	17.3%
Europe	12.3%	38.9%
Oceana	0.5%	53.5%
N. America	5.1%	69.7%
Total	**100%**	—

In Africa, with over 14% of the world's population (about 1 person in 7), less than 4% have access to the internet. In Asia, with over half the world's population, only slightly over 10% have internet access. This seemingly low Asian percentage (in an area known for high technology development) could be related to the presence within the total Asian continent of large countries with both high (Japan, South Korea) and relatively low (India, Indonesia, Phillipines) internet development (See Table

6.2 below). The Middle East and South America both currently have relatively low percentages of access. Europe and the United States both have relatively high percentages of access. Oceana could possibly be an aberration, perhaps caused by the unique geography of the area and its relatively small population.

Table 6.2: Countries with Over 50 mm Population with High and Low Internet Usage Rates

> 50% i/n usage (mm usage/mm pop'n)	< 10% i/n usage (mm usage/mm pop'n)
USA (211/302)	India (40/1,130)
Japan (86/129)	Indonesia (18/224)
Germany (50/83)	Pakistan (12/168)
UK (38/60)	Phillipines (8/87)
S. Korea (34/51)	Nigeria (5/162)
France (31/61)	Egypt (5/72)
Italy (31/60)	Bangladesh(< 1/137)
	Myanmar (< 1/54)
Total (481/746) = 64.4%	Total (88/2,034) = 4.3%
% total world usage: 43.7%	% total world usage: 8.0%
% total world pop'n: 7.8%	% total world pop'n: 32.5%

Table 6.2 above looks separately at large countries (over 50 million in population) with either high (left column) or low (right column) degrees of internet usage among their people. The Table presents in parenthesis first the reported internet usage for the country, then the population of the country. It shows vast current disparities in proportionate usage among large countries—with seven countries (corresponding to almost 1/3 of the world's population, 32.5%—bottom of right column) having an average usage penetration (usage number divided by population number) of only 4.3% and together representing only 8.0% of the world's total internet usage. Conversely technologically more advanced countries with only 7.8% of the world's population (left column) have almost two thirds (64.4%) using the internet, together representing 43.7% of the world's total of internet usage. China currently has 14.8% of the world's useage—therefore not appearing in Table 6.2.

Another way of looking at the Miniwatts data is to compare *current usage rates* within the various areas with *growth in that area's usage*. Table 6.3 addresses this perspective.

Table 6.3: Usage vs. Growth

Region	i/n usage, yr 2007	growth 2000-07
Africa	2.0%	638%
Middle East	3.0%	491%
S. America	8.0%	433%
Europe	29.0%	200%
N. America	21.0%	116%

This data points to a *basically inverse relationship* between the percentage of the area's population using the internet in the year 2007 and the percentage growth of those numbers over what they were in the year 2000. Of course the smaller usage areas were forming the growth percentages on a smaller base, representing some distortion of the overall impression. Nevertheless I believe the trend possibly points to at least some "leveling out" in the future and to the possibility that—to the degree that use of the internet often *contributes* to the development of individual Post Culture by expanding potential connectivity and available data—geography could become less of a factor in influencing the development of Post Culturality than it might be now.

The Emergence of Post Culture

Data in the previous section could lead to anticipation of a day when access to the internet and ability to use it for increased connectivity and information could be less concentrated among those who happen to live in more advanced countries than it is now. I believe the arrival of that time could produce an impact on some potential immigrants to America. This is because many more could, if they wish, *begin earlier* on developing a *more cosmopolitan, less traditional outlook*—characteristics that could prove useful in easing their transition to the relatively open society of America by allowing some to move more easily beyond their previous more bounded cultures—to more easily approach over time the Post Cultural condition. The central concept of *cosmopolitanism* which I would like to use in this discussion was articulated by Hannerz in 1990 as: ". . . an intellectual and aesthetic stance of openness toward divergent cultural experiences, a search for contrasts rather than uniformity" (p. 240).

Everyone with internet access does not become cosmopolitan. Additionally I believe it is possible to become cosmopolitan reacting to other contextual and experiential factors, not necessarily only the internet. Important and formative experiences could also come from work or life, from friendships with unusual people or from exposure to media such as radio, television and motion pictures which present appealing characters, beliefs, ways of life and values for possible appropriation. A *cosmopolitan outlook* can be encouraged by exposure to information, artifacts, goods and information that freely circulate around the world ignoring borders and pre-existing cultural boundaries.

One way of experiencing unfamiliar cultural input is to travel to different places. In Chapter ONE I showed that fully 3% of the world's population presently comprises migrants—those living in a different country (and in many of these instances a different culture) from that where they were born—a number approaching 200 million people. Bammer (1994), quoting Sutter (1990), estimates the number of refugees (displaced persons who are part of the migrant flow) to be at least 60 million in the period since 1945. The World Health Organization estimates that leisure and business travelers made more than 800 million international journeys worldwide in 2006 alone, most returning to their homes after the trip (See Footnote 6.4). Whether voluntary or forced, whether one way or round trip these voyages allowed for the experiencing of new worlds, new people, new ways of life and a possible weakening or breakdown of the conception held by some that nothing of significance or value existed beyond their neighborhood.

Before the internet there were so-called "conventional" media which have continually played a role in breaking down traditional cultures and in encouraging cosmopolitanism around the world. Let us briefly examine some of these.

Newspapers have been bringing news of unusual events and attractive people to the literate public since 1605, when the first newspaper, believed by many scholars to be the German language *Relation aller Fuernemmen und gedenckwuerdigen Historien* (*Collection of all distinguished and commemorable news)* was published in Strassburg (See Footnote 6.5). Wire services, such as Associated Press have since 1846 documented events in lands far distant from the reader, introducing ways of life that many found new and exotic (See Footnote 6.6). I believe these services played an important role in broadening the traditional role of newspapers which was binding people to their localities by reporting local news—opening up new vistas to some degree. Today, The World Association of Newspapers reports that 395 million people worldwide buy a newspaper every day (up from 374 million in 1999) and that more than one billion people read a newspaper daily (See Footnote 6.7). About half a century after newspapers magazines began to appear as a specialized media format, carrying information of interest to specific sub-audiences. Today literally thousands of magazine titles are published around the world, bringing updates for some readers, totally new ideas to others.

In 1896 the electronic era of modern media began, when Marconi was granted a patent for what we know as radio, going on to start the first primitive radio station the following year (See Footnote 6.8). Navia and Zweifel (2004), quoting World Bank data, report that in 2004 there were 293 radios for every 1,000 inhabitants worldwide. Electronic television as we know it began in the United States in 1936 and, by 1939 had also appeared in Germany, The United Kingdom, France, Poland, The Soviet Union, Japan and Italy (See Footnote 6.9), spreading around the world from there. Navia and Zweifel (ibid) report a current period worldwide average television penetration of 150 sets per thousand inhabitants. In my many years in the advertising field, in America, Europe and Asia, I came to consider electronic media as particularly effective in quickly and pro-actively transferring the listener or viewer to an imagined world where he could, for a time, experience a life very different from what surrounded him physically.

All of these so called conventional media, even though today thought of by many as somehow not modern nevertheless began and continued a process of bringing the world into one's living room. In the words of Tomlinson (1999): ". . . the paradigmatic experience of global modernity for most people . . . is that of staying in one place but experiencing the displacement (movement to a different place) that global modernity brings to them" (p. 9). Tomlinson continues by saying: "The experience connected with the routine use of media technologies must be counted as one of the most significant and widely available sources of cultural deterritorialization—indirect travel" (p. 202).

Writing in 2006, Shohat adds this point:

> . . . within postmodern culture, the media not only set agendas and
> frame debates but also inflect desire, memory and fantasy. The con-

temporary media shape identity; indeed many argue that they now exist close to the very core of identity production. (p. 307)

In the next section I will return to the literature and show how additional scholars with diverse perspectives articulate the process by which cultural diffusion—the spread of information, images and possibilities for appropriation around the world—leads to the breakdown of bounded traditional cultures and prepares the way for many to experience a new Post Cultural condition.

Scholars Discuss Cultural Diffusion and the Breakdown of Tradition

One of the more prominent and comprehensive recent models of cultural diffusion and the breakdown of tradition is that of Apparadai. In *Modernity at Large: Cultural Dimensions of Globalization* (1996) he identifies media and migrations as two basic ingredients for breakdown. He advises (p. 9): ". . . only in the past two decades or so (have) media and migration become so globalized, that is to say, active across large and irregular transnational terrains." Even though Apparadai is mainly talking about the broader process of globalization, his thoughts are useful in understanding the dynamics that lead to a Post Cultural condition. He proposes "an elementary framework" for exploring relationships among five dimensions of global cultural flows (ibid), characterized as types of landscapes. These are specified as follows:

> *Ethnoscapes* are ". . . the landscapes of persons who constitute the shifting world in which we live: tourists, immigrants, refugees, exiles, guest workers and other moving groups and individuals (who) constitute an essential feature of the hitherto world and appear to affect the politics of (and between) nations to an unprecedented degree. . . . *Technoscapes* refer to the global configuration . . . of technology and the fact that technology, both high and low, both mechanical and informational, now moves at high speeds across various kinds of previously impervious boundaries. . . . *Financescapes* refer to currency markets, national stock exchanges and commodity speculations (which) move megamonies through national turnstiles at blinding speed, with vast, absolute implications for small differences in percentage points and time units. . . . *Mediascapes* . . . refer both to the distribution of the electronic capabilities to produce and disseminate information (news-

papers, magazines, television stations and film-production studios) which are now available to a growing number of private and public interests throughout the world and to the images of the world created by these media. . . . (Finally) *Ideascapes* are also concatenations of images, but they are often directly political and frequently have to do with . . . ideologies. . . . (pp. 34-36)

Apparadai's vision of the implications of the interworkings of his five "scapes" is that the individual is encouraged to imagine new worlds and new forms of relationship freed from the bonds of previous culture. Apparadai's thinking is reviewed by fellow Anthropologist Ted C. Lewellen who, in *The Anthropology of Globalization* (2002) writes:

In Appadurai's imagery . . . patterns overlap, flow and are transformed to create ever new and more complex patterns of interaction and thought. For example, mass migration is normative in world history, but when conjoined with the electronic media—television, radio, movies and the Internet—new patterns emerge. Whereas in the past, imagination was the property of the artist, the shaman, the poet, and the scholar, imagination is now part of everybody's everyday life. Mass media creates new scripts for possible lives and possible futures. The limits of what can be conceived, of what is possible, have been enormously extended. (p. 96)

There are many other articulations of the effects which modern technologies have had on traditional cultures, both in America and in other countries, allowing for a Post Cultural condition to begin to emerge. As early as 1991 Giddens commented as follows:

. . . we live 'in the world' in a different sense from previous eras of history. Everyone still continues to live a local life, and the constraints of the body ensure that all individuals, at every moment, are contextually situated in time and space. Yet the transformations of place, and the intrusion of distance into local activities, combined with the centrality of mediated experience radically change what 'the world' actually is. . . . Although everyone lives a local life, phenomenal worlds for the most part are truly global . . . in very few instances does the phenomenal world any longer correspond to the habitual setting through which an individual physically moves. (p. 37)

Writing in 1999, Tomlinson stated:

. . . People's phenomenal world(s)—come to include distant events and processes more routinely in their perceptions of what is significant for their own personal lives. Deterritorialization involves the ever-broadening horizon of relevance in people's routine experience, removing not only general 'cultural awareness' but, crucially, the processes of individual 'life planning' from a self-contained context centered on physical locality or politically defined territory . . . (the) choice provided by new media technologies contributes to deterritorialization. Being 'better informed' implies having available a range of perspectives on events beyond that of the 'home culture', being able to situate oneself at a distance from the (national, local) 'viewpoint'. Whatever this may promise for the development of cosmopolitan cultural dispositions, it also represents a loss of the cultural certainty, even of the existential 'comfort' involved in having the world 'out there' presented to us from the still point of an unchallenged national/local perspective. . . . (p. 116)

A sociological perspective is added by Eade, writing in 1997, who notes:

. . . an emphasis on boundedness and coherence traditionally dominated the sociological treatment of the idea of culture, particularly in the functionalist tradition where collective meaning construction was dealt with largely as serving the purposes of social integration. So a 'culture' parallels the problematic notion of 'a society' as a bounded entity occupying a physical territory mapped as a political territory (predominantly the nation-state) and binding individual meaning constructions into this circumscribed social, political space. The connectivity of globalization is clearly threatening to such conceptualizations, not only because the multiform penetration of localities breaks into this binding of meanings to place but because it undermines the thinking through which culture and fixity of location are originally paired. (p. 25)

Garcia Canclini (1995) discusses the phenomenon with reference to "emerging countries" such as his native Mexico:

We have gone from societies dispersed in thousands of peasant communities with traditional, local and homogeneous cultures—in some regions with strong indigenous roots, with little communication with the rest of each nation—to a largely urban scheme with a heterogeneous symbolic offering renewed by a constant interaction of the local with national and transnational networks of communication. . . . How can we explain the fact that many changes in thinking and taste in urban life coincide with those in the peasantry, if not because of commercial interactions of the latter with the cities and reception of electronic media in rural houses which connects them with modern innovations. (p. 207)

Garcia Canclini continues:

. . . the interactions of new technologies with previous culture makes them part of a much bigger project. . . . Although many works remain within the minority or popular circuits for which they were made, the prevailing trend is for all sectors to mix into their tastes objects whose points of origin were previously separated. (p. 228)

Finally he adds:

There is an implosion of the third world into the first. The notion of an authentic culture as an autonomous internally coherent universe is no longer sustainable, except as a 'useful fiction' or a revealing distortion. (p. 217)

Tomlinson (ibid p. 71) quotes Hannerz (1990):

. . . the world has become one network of social relationships and between its different regions there is a flow of meanings as well as a flow of people and goods. (p. 237)

Tomlinson (ibid) goes on to say:

. . . (in) the individual's 'phenomenal world': people probably come to include distant events and processes more routinely in their perceptions of what is significant for their own personal lives. This is one aspect of what deterritorialization may involve: the ever broadening horizon of relevance in people's routine experience, removing not only general 'cultural awareness' but crucially, the processes of individual 'life planning' from a self-contained context centered on physical locality or politically defined territory. (p. 115)

Morley and Robins (1995) add:

. . . we should reject all images of 'pure, internally homogeneous, authentic, indigenous culture(s) and recognize that every culture has, in fact, ingested foreign elements from exogenous sources, with the various elements gradually becoming 'naturalized' within it. (p. 129)

I will close this array of perspectives on cultural breakdown with these words from Kahn (1995). In *Culture, Multiculture, Postculture* he observes:

> . . . in challenging the fixity of cultural boundaries . . . discoveries serve to preserve the myth of the cultural center . . . centers, like boundaries, become arbitrary points in cultural space, acquiring their significance only when something outside of that infinite variation is imposed, thus defining this or that point as the focus of cultural purity. (p. 130)

It seems to me that, in one way or another, each of the quotes above contributes to the idea that often new or unusual information, sometimes emanating from a far away source and speaking of new and different ways of life, weakens ties to traditional culture, thereby reducing the exclusive reliance on pre-existing cultural prisms for the viewing and interpretation of contextual or interpersonal change.

Post Culture and Early Backgrounds: A Case of Contrasts

Previously in this chapter I introduced the construct of *Post Culturality* as I intended to use it. Reprising this material: "In the *Post Cultural Orientation* all semblance of bounded cultures has disappeared. . . . I define a *post cultural* person as one who can *perceive and react to contextual and interpersonal changes fluidly—an orientation favoured by the various conditions that the person might have experienced*" (p. 82). I also indicated my feeling that it is not absolutely necessary to have worked extensively with and become comfortable with advanced information technology in order to become Post Cultural. However I believe that the instant worldwide connectivity, easy access to great amounts of information and general speeding up of interactions that are enabled by the internet and derivative communications technologies over a long period of time become an advantage.

I believe that my teenage daughter Nicole and I have both more or less achieved—or at least approached—the Post Cultural condition as defined above, although starting out from vastly different early environments. Her case was mediated by the forces of modern information technology, mine by diverse life experiences accumulated over many years.

To add texture to the discussion I will present in this section a matched pair of portraits of some every day life activities of my daughter and myself when we were the same age, timeframes that were of course years apart in real time. The 1952 material below shows pieces of my own life as a 12 year old (as I remember it) growing up in a college town (Ithaca, NY) in mid twentieth century America. 2007 will show corresponding pieces of Nicole's life when she was 12 years old growing up now in another, similar college town (Princeton, NJ) early in the twenty-first century. Whereas she had full access to the technologies of social saturation (as they are now defined) I did not. My intent is to show how our lives were experientially different at that life stage and relate that difference to our similarity in outlooks now.

1952—Marvin's Story

My mother was a housewife, almost always home and able to serve dinner at about 5 PM each night. After dinner I did my homework without the aid of the electronic devices available to virtually every American student today. I did the laborious calculations of my math homework by hand (There were no calculators in those days). Then I waited. When 7 PM finally arrived (the time when the one available television station started broadcasting) I could sit in front of our twelve inch, black and white television set screen for a few hours watching grainy transmissions of programming which invariably presented a picture of a bounded, singular culture before going to bed. Still, this was a big change from a period only two years earlier when no one in our neighborhood, including ourselves, had a television set at all and the evening's entertainment comprised the family sitting around the living room sharing the experience of listening to the radio. In 1952 we had recently also experienced an advance in our telephone capability. Before this we had shared a party line with several neighbors, never knowing when we would be able to call out or receive calls and knowing that any who wanted to could invade our privacy by listening in on our phone conversations. While we still had only one telephone handset we now had our own phone line. We could call out or receive calls anytime. For the most part we only made calls to friends and relatives in our town, long distance calls to places further away being in those days considerably more expensive. We wanted to capture important family moments then, as we do now. To take still pictures we had an enormous, fixed focus box camera. The cumbersome operating procedure involved inserting film, taking pictures until the film exposures available were exhausted, then removing the film, taking it to a local shop for processing and receiving it back in a few weeks. For moving pictures we had a primitive 8mm film camera that needed to be wound up with a crank. The processing procedures were similar to those for still pictures. We did not have the ability to record sound to accompany the grainy, often disjointed images that appeared when the developed film was eventually shown at home. The limited world I lived in every day extended also to travel, which was usually by car or sometimes train. Car trips were normally to locations in or around our home in Ithaca. Occasional trips to New York City for holidays and other special occasions were usually by train—the trip being constructed as a substantial journey, even though the actual distance was then as it is now only about 200 miles, a distance we would today consider short.

2007—Nicole's Story

By comparison, my daughter Nicole's life at the same chronological age was relatively complicated, more externally connected, faster moving and full of options. When she came home from school (where she had spent the day mostly studying topics I did not encounter until I reached high school or, in some cases, even college) Nicole could watch any one of 300 cable tv channels, presenting programming in a wide variety of genres and cultural traditions, on a 42 inch high-definition television set. Having gone to Japanese language school on weekends since age four and having lived her entire life in a bi-lingual Japanese-English household she was completely fluent in Japanese and had a choice not only between programming genres but between English language and Japanese language programs. The Japanese television was delivered either live or tape delayed from Tokyo via satellite—the same programs that were aired the same day in Japan—thus transporting herself in her imagination half way around the world. If she wanted to she could tape any program in either language for viewing later. She sometimes watched pre-recorded programming such as movies or instructional videos on DVDs or VHS tapes. She often sent and received e mails and instant messages on her own laptop computer, establishing instant connectivity with those of her friends in compatible time zones. Or when appropriate she could communicate on a time-altered basis with those in Europe or Japan. She often attached to e mails documents that were available in electronic format, including coloured pictures. She sometimes initiated or received streamed videos over the internet. After dinner Nicole used the internet for doing her homework—taking only a few minutes to accomplish research that would have taken me weeks to do manually. Using the search engine Google she could enter a keyword and almost instantly find on her screen a broad variety of websites from all over the world that deal with that topic—some in English and some in other languages. Reaching any website she wanted to explore could be done with one or two clicks. When she was finished she often relaxed by playing games on her computer which were either embedded in her computer's hard disk or alternatively could be downloaded from seemingly thousands of internet sites. She and her friends often played internet games against each other, each from her own home using her own laptop computer, by logging onto the same website. She could also play against complete strangers who happened to be logged on to the game site at that time. We have three telephone handsets in our home, two of which are cordless and can be carried anywhere in the house for additional privacy. These are connected to the same high speed cable that provides our broadband internet service—assuring high quality, low cost telephone access to anywhere in the world (Nicole can talk to her friends in Japan for hours, experiencing quality levels similar to calling just down the street, for US$3 per hour—an amount that corresponded to the cost of only one minute of US-Japan telephone airtime as recently as 20 years ago). One of our handsets is also connected to a fax machine. And we have our choice of several different phone answering machines to use when we are out, so we never miss calls. Additionally Nicole has her own cellular phone, as do my wife and myself. Thus she is virtually always potentially in touch with her parents and friends. Her cellular phone has other uses, such as playing games that are embedded in it or for text messaging. Nicole has her own conventional style film camera, that can be used in preference to low cost disposable cameras that are readily available almost anywhere in the US. However, usually she uses her digital camera, which produces high quality pictures that are instantly viewable (and errors accordingly correctible). These digital images can be sent anywhere in the world via the internet and arrive in seconds. We can, and often do, receive other people's digital images, sent to us over the internet.

Additionally the digital camera can be used as a video camera, recording sound as well and replacing a traditional Super-8 VHS camcorder which we had for many years—itself a former revolutionary improvement over historic conventional home movie cameras. The digital camera, of course, does not use film. Its electronic output pictures can be printed on either regular or specialized computer printers. Because of our family history and international connectedness my daughter may have done more traveling than some of her contemporaries. However, it is not unusual today for children to travel vast distances by plane. Nicole has made 11 trips to Japan and visited many countries in Western Europe, including The Netherlands, England, France, Germany, Austria and Italy. She is familiar with a number of the top museums in Europe, such as The Rijksmuseum, The Louvre and The British Museum as well as many other important European cultural sites. She has also made two trips to Hawaii. The sophistication she has developed from this travel exposure to other cultures, added to her bi-lingual daily living context dwarfs the sense I had when her age of the world outside of neighborhood, town and maybe state. Now, when she goes to Japan or makes other long trips she often travels alone.

Different Routes, Same Destination

Now still only fourteen years old it is difficult to predict how Nicole will eventually develop. What I can say now from observation is that bi-culturality (Japanese and American) for her has been a stage en route to Post Culturality. However I believe that the types of adjustment described in this book—Mono-Cultural, Assimilationist, Separation, Hyphenated Identity, Bi-Cultural, Hybrid Cultural and Post Cultural—are not necessarily arrayed in a linear sequence for everyone. Rather I feel they are conditions that any individual seeking adjustment can relate to *on an individual basis* at any time, moving from one to another as seems appropriate.

That question aside, how is it that father and daughter with such different childhoods could both approach the Post Cultural condition—as individuals who can relate to changing contexts and interpersonal situations directly, without the intervening mediation of particularized culture? In Nicole's case she has had exposure to a wide variety of cultures and at the same time has grown familiar with, and is comfortable with, modern information technology. In my own case I have absorbed aspects of many different cultures through living in countries other than America for many years at a time, through my marriage to a Japanese and through my business experiences where I have at various times played the role of entrepreneur, business owner, manager in large organizational settings, consultant, educator, writer and student. In these various roles I have worked in, or at least had exposure to 45 different businesses all over the world. I have become Post Cultural over a long period by the steady accumulation of life experience rather than operating on the compressed schedule of one who lives a large part of life in the electronically mediated world of information technology. Both Nicole and I contemplate a state of Post Culturality, although having travelled by somewhat different routes to get there.

Perspectives on Post Culture

When I started writing this chapter I had pictured a relationship that did not prove out completely. I understood the technologies of social saturation. It was not difficult to document their growth, elaboration or (decreasing) unevenness of international development, particularly the internet. Nor was it particularly difficult to find the quotes of scholars who related the breakdown of traditional cultures to the general international advance of technology, whether the internet was included or not. However I had imagined relationship to information technology to be a more intense endogenous phenomenon that came *by itself* in time to dominate some people to the point where their cultural anchoring, as I have used the term in the Chapter THREE discussion of ACES, would be to a degree displaced—in other words, my original idea had been that the internet was the key to understanding cultural disintegration in many cases. That could still be true for some people. However, in the focused discussions I had about it, and reflecting on my own and my daughter's life experiences, it was not consistently demonstrated. I now believe my original idea was too simplistic and in need of re-formulation.

I have come to regard Post Culturality as a condition that is developed through exposure to intense amounts of new and unusual information, *which could come in many forms*. It could be in the form of encounters on the internet, real or imagined travels to new lands, appropriations of new life styles observed directly or through electronic or other media or in other ways. Based on what I have seen and read it seems that the main commonality that runs through conditions of preparedness for Post

Culturality is what Hannerz, quoted earlier in describing *cosmopolitanism*, observed as ". . . an intellectual and aesthetic stance of openness toward divergent cultural experiences . . ." This then allows for the regarding of contextual or interpersonal changes directly, without the mediating influence of particular culture. My belief, in other words, is that cosmopolitanism (as defined by Hannerz) tends to enable Post Culture. We saw in the preceding chapter how Hybrid Culturality began by building pieces onto a stable base identity. Post Culture then might be contemplated as a more extreme version where the stable base identity has also, in effect, disappeared.

Chapter SEVEN

Summary and Reflections

I started out in my Preface asking the question "Who are you?" I pointed out that the answer—whether it is simply one's name or more profoundly one's identity—was inexorably linked to both context and relevant individual mode of adaptation, at least that operative at the time. When I started out I intended the question to be mainly directed toward American immigrants. However, as I have developed the ideas in this book I realize that they are more broadly applicable. For anyone can move into and out of the modes of adaptation I have covered. They are not conceived as being permanent, nor are they stages through which one moves in a linear fashion, as in many theories of personality development.

America is known—rightfully—as a country built by immigrants. Immigrants have come to America for many different reasons. Some were seeking freedom from physical or intellectual persecution. Some were fleeing war or famine. Some were seeking a setting where they could start a new life, characterized by economic or lifestyle opportunity. Some came to join family members who were already here. One thing that most had in common was that they found in America a place that was probably quite unlike wherever they had come from. Pursuing a fulfilling life in America involved individual choices about strategies likely to accomplish what they had set out to do.

I have constructed American acculturational development history in the form of periods—beginning my story with a time late in the eighteenth century when predominantly white immigrants largely from England, Germany and other countries in Northern Europe came here in considerable numbers, bringing with them a more or less contained, rural, Protestant culture to continue to follow as best they could while developing the new land. They had been preceded by groups we know today as Native Americans—felt by many scholars to have migrated to America from Asia over the land bridge that existed thousands of years ago and is now below the level of the Bering Sea—groups that migrated southward when they were able, to form tribes many of which continue to exist today throughout North, Central and South America. While there was some mixing of American white settlers with the tribes that were here in the territory that eventually became The United States often this mixing had an adverse result, such as European diseases destroying substantial parts of Native American Indian populations, wars and other negative results. On balance the groups largely remained apart, basically distrusting each other, often warring against each other and generally preferring to maintain their respective traditional ways of life. A third group with a separate and discernable culture comprised the Negro slaves who were initially captured in Africa and brought to America to work in adverse conditions as the economy of the American South developed. Even though displaced from their original cultures the slaves were, for the most part, not welcomed into the white society that prevailed in the areas where they were. In short, this was an era when the three main groups—each clearly different culturally from the others—did not fully integrate with each other. And acculturation, as I have used the term in this book (meaning the process of adjustment to stresses brought on by prolonged contact with unusual or different cultures), was in my view of limited importance in American life at that time. This period is discussed in Chapter ONE.

Beginning around 1880 a change in the character of the immigrant flow to America became evident. In response to deteriorating conditions in many parts of Europe, many "new" immigrants came not from Northern Europe but from Central and Southern Europe. These immigrants were culturally much different from those who came before—often Catholic or Jewish rather than Protestant, speaking languages and following conventions of food, clothing and inter-personal relationships that seemed unusual to the previous settlers, and embracing a basically urban rather than rural lifestyle. The substantial presence of these new groups, who at least shared a European origin, led to considerable stress at the time including discrimination against the new immigrants by the old—presenting what was in my view America's first large-scale need for acculturational definition. Scholars throughout the country debated the future of America—whether it would develop as a heterogeneous mixture of different peoples or whether the result would be a plural situation where each of many cultures maintained its essential features. As this debate was going on a play entitled *The Melting Pot* opened in New York—a play that was to have substantial impact in that its assimilationist message of a single America came to define the aspirations of many immigrants. Of course, not all attempted to fit into the mold of a single America. Some chose other adjustment strategies, such as Separation into groups that maintained the previous culture and Hyphenated Identities which blended new and old cultures but with each preserving a prominent place in day to day life. But many did identify with the Melting Pot idea and the construct, defined in the period of the late nineteenth and early twentieth centuries remains popular in some places today. This period is discussed in Chapter TWO.

In 1965 there was a major alteration in US immigration laws. Among other changes, a country quota system for potential immigrants, which had been put in place some forty years before, was dismantled and many more were free to emigrate to America. A largely unexpected consequence of this change in legal framework was that American immigration surged, while also changing in origin. In the ensuing period, rather than immigrants tending to come from Europe, most came from Latin America and the Far East. These tended to adopt a quite different strategy for acculturation and adjustment to America. Rather than aspire to assimilate into American life they tended to choose the development of an American personality while also maintaining their original personality—a condition called bi-culturality, allowing for either formation to rise to the surface as desired. A cohort of social scientists came to prominence studying this phenomenon and such related issues as whether personality development was inherently a uni-dimensional or multi-dimensional (orthogonal) process and whether new immigrant cultures could make a lasting impact on receiving cultures already established in the new land. A fuller discussion of this material can be found in Chapters TWO and THREE.

These issues came to be resolved through the work of, among others, Canadian cross-cultural psychologist John Berry in a model of adjustment which he developed late in the twentieth century. Feeling that the Berry model, while useful in many respects, was not as powerful as it could be in placing immigrants in acculturational space I developed a framework, described in Chapter THREE, which I called ACES—an acronym for Anchoring, Communication, Enjoyment and Sensitivity, variables my experience suggested were important for adjustment. My ACES framework is designed to complement the Berry acculturational model in defining the degree to which an individual is bi-cultural. Chapter FOUR describes how Hispanic and Far Eastern immigrants play the bi-cultural game of life in America, using narratives of composite individuals taken from real life (but remaining anonymous) examples. I use the Berry model and ACES framework to determine whether particular individuals featured in the constructed narratives had moved into the space of full bi-culturality—a condition where the individual is essentially able to act in each cultural role as if uni-cultural in that culture, reacting to changing contexts and relationships without undue influence from the non-active alternate personality. Once again it is important to understand that not all Hispanic or Far Eastern immigrants follow an acculturational strategy of bi-culturality. The strategy is contemplated as the modal method of adjustment for those groups, but adjustment is still an individual matter.

In Chapter FIVE I deal with Hybrid Culturality as an adjustment strategy, using the situations of immigrant Muslims to illustrate the point. In this condition, a strong base identity is elaborated by the addition of pieces of other personalities and modes of adjustment observed and appropriated for use as desired in an *individually appropriate blended mix*. In the Muslim case these pieces could come from exposure to other Muslims who come from different backgrounds, from non-Muslim Americans, from media or from other sources.

In Chapter SIX I begin discussing the technologies of social saturation described by Gergen in 1991. Essentially comprising a revolution in information and media technology that has grown massively since then these technologies have helped many individuals develop *Post Culturally*—an orientation which I have characterized as engendering the ability to react to contextual or interpersonal changes fluidly, an orientation favoured by the various conditions which the person might have experienced. I review relevant literature and show through comparisons within my own family that the technologies under discussion, while helpful, are not absolutely necessary to allow a Post Cultural profile to develop.

While many of the phases I have discussed were initiated by specific contextual modifications situated in time, such as changes in immigration origin points driven by conditions in Europe or new US immigration laws the acculturational development phase constructs are not intended as contained segments that necessarily start and stop at defined times. Nor are they intended as a linear sequence that individuals must move through. Rather, the phases are modal adjustment strategies of individual immigrants—not all immigrants at that time but rather those who believe that the particular strategy is then right for them. In some cases it is not difficult to imagine how an immigrant embracing, for example, Hybrid Culturality could move into Post Cultural space later or for other movements to occur. As always, adjustment is an individual matter, expressed individually according to forces in play at that particular time.

Reflections

I have approached the writing of this book not as someone who has spent a lifetime as a social scientist but as a businessman with a background in the social science field—far distant in time but of abiding significance. Much of my work in the business world involved studying behavior patterns of consumers, making judgements of how they would react to marketing strategies and tactics. That concern was a major factor in my choosing acculturation as a topic to write about.

For many years I was active as a consultant, lecturer and writer in the field of marketing to Hispanic consumers. This field has grown significantly in recent years and I am proud of the part I played in developing the specialized methods needed to reach and satisfy the needs of this group. I became aware of acculturation status being of extreme importance in constructing marketing strategies for Hispanics as this variable often governs the type of media that the individual is exposed to, the kinds of products that would or would not be of interest, the kinds of advertising that would be most effective in producing action, the nature of the people who would influence purchase decisions and other similar factors. In seeking to improve my ability as a marketer of products and services to Hispanics I came to be aware of the relative lack of materials discussing acculturation as a social process, as opposed to simply talking about action correlates. So I set out to at least start to fill some of this vacuum in my doctoral work, from which this book is derived.

Some years ago I wrote an article entitled *Dehomogenized Marketing for the Twenty-First Century* in which I argued that the white, suburban, middle class consumer who formed the core of the idealized target for many American product and service companies would, based on demographic changes that were then beginning to surface, become a minority. Conversely, groups then considered minorities would ascend in aggregate into the majority, with the consequence that America would become a place where one size no longer fitted all, or even most. Since then I have witnessed the continued growth of non-mainstream groups and a new interest in more exotic, non-mainstream cultures. I believe these trends will continue and I intend to do my best to put what I have learned in writing this document to use in spreading a greater understanding of the non-traditional condition in America.

Endnotes

Chapter ONE

1.1. See http://en.wikipedia.org/wiki/Immigration_to_the_United_States, p. 2

1.2. 1790 American populations from other origin countries/areas (000): Africa 757, Netherlands 100, France 15, Sweden 2. Source: (same as Footnote 1.1 above)

1.3. For Immigration Act of May 26, 1924, see: http://www.uscis.gov/graphics/shared/aboutus/statistics/legishist/470.htm

For Immigration and Nationality Act of June 27, 1952 see: http://www,uscis.gov/graphics/shared/aboutus/statistics/legishist/511.htm

For Immigration and Nationality Act Amendments, as of October 3, 1965, see: http://www.uscis.gov/graphics/shared/aboutus/statistics/legishist/526.htm

Chapter FOUR

4.1. Source: e mail, S. Palacios to M. Shaub, 26 December 2005. Yankelovich and Company is a prominent market research firm. In the last few years they have partnered with Cheskin in a longitudinal study dealing with Hispanic attitudes and certain aspects of consumer behavior.

4.2. From corporate tutorial presentation, see Valdes, I. in References section.

Chapter FIVE

5.1. This section was compiled from three sources. These covered basically the same material but from different perspectives. The first source, Kronemer and Wolfe (2002) was a documentary program developed for viewing on US Public Television. The second source was Wormser (1994), pp. 16-19. The third was a presentation by Mr. Moustafa Zayyed, an Islamic scholar and expert on the life of Muhammed.

5.2. See: http://en.wikipedia.org/wiki/Ottoman_Empire, p.4; and
http://en.wikipedia.org/wiki/Muhammed, p.1

Chapter SIX

6.1. From the website http://www.internetworldstats.com/stats.htm. The site is maintained by Miniwatts Marketing Group. Data is current as of March 2007. Sources of data are www.world-gazeteer.com, Nielsen//NetRatings, ITU and Computer Industry Almanac.

6.2. See: http://www.paulallen.net/2005/12/06/2-billion-cell-phones-in-use/

6.3. See: http://www.myrateplan.com/sat/international-programming-on-satellite-TV.php

6.4. See: http://www.who.int/bookorders/anglais/detart1.jsp?sesslan=1&codlan=1&codlan=18&co

6.5. See: http://en.wikipedia.org/wiki/Johann_Carolus

6.6. See: http://en.wikipedia.org/wiki/Associated.Press

6.7. See: http://www.wan-press.org/article7321.html

6.8. See http://en.wikipedia.org/wiki/radio

6.9. See http://en.wikipedia.org/wiki/Timeline_of_the_introduction_of_television_in_countries

Bibliography

Abdalati, H. (1988), *Islam in Focus*, New Delhi: Millat Book Centre.

Afridi, S. (2001), *Muslims in America: Identity, diversity and the challenge of understanding,* NY: Carnegie Corporation.

Ali, A. Y. (1998), *The Qur'aan, translation,* Islamic Educational Services, Mt. Holly, NJ.

Antioch University Multicultural Center: (website) http://www.multi culturalcenter.org/test/test_titles16.cfm.

Appadurai, A. (1996), *Modernity at Large: cultural dimensions of globalization,* Minneapolis: University of Minnesota Press.

Bammer, A. (Ed) (1994), *Displacements: cultural identities in question,* Bloomington: University of Indiana Press.

Barnett, H. G. (1941), *Yearbook of the American Philosophical Society,* New York.

Barone, M. (2001), *The New Americans: how the melting pot can work again,* Washington, DC: Regnery Publishing, Inc.

Barrett, F. J. & Fry, R. E. (2005), *Appreciative Inquiry,* Chagrin Falls, OH: Taos Institute Publications.

Bell, L. (2007), "Customers, Creativity and Branding," in *DMNews,* taken from website: http://www.dmnews.com/cms/dm-news/shows-assns/42730.html.

Berry, J. W. (2003), "Conceptual Approaches to Acculturation," in K. M. Chun, P. Balls Organista and G. Marin (Eds), *Acculturation: Advances in Theory, Measurement and Applied Research,* Washington, DC: American Psychological Association.

Berry, J. W. & Sam, D. (1997), "Acculturation and Adaptation," in J. W. Berry, M. H. Segall and C. Kagitcibasi (Eds), *Handbook of cross-cultural psychology,* Vol. 3, Social Behaviour and Applications, (pp. 291-326), Boston: Allyn and Bacon.

Booth, W. (1998), "One Nation Indivisible: Is It History?" In *The Washington Post*, 22 February 1998, reprinted in website: http://www.washingtonpost.com/wp-srv/national/longterm/meltingpot/melt0222.htm.

Bronfenbrenner, U. (1979), *Ecology of Human Development: experiments by nature and design,* Cambridge, MA: Harvard University Press.

Caetano, R. (1987), "Acculturation and Drinking Patterns Among U. S. Hispanics," *British Journal of Addiction* 82, pp. 789-799.

Canclini, N. G. (1995), *Hybrid Cultures: Strategies for Entering and Leaving Modernity,* Minneapolis: University of Minnesota Press.

Candelaria, Cordelia Chavez, Executive Ed. (2004), *Encyclopedia of Latino Popular Culture,* Westport, CT: Greenwood Press.

Cateura, L. B. (2005), *Voices of American Muslims: 23 profiles*, New York: Hippocrene Books.

Cesari, J. (2004), "Islam in the West: Modernity and Globalization Revisited," in Schaebler, B. and Sternberg, L. (Eds) (2004), *Globalization and the Muslim World: culture, religion and modernity (Modern intellectual and political history of the Middle East),* Syracuse, NY: Syracuse University Press.

Chun, K. M., Balls Organista, P. and Marin, G. (Eds) (2003), *Acculturation Advances in Theory, Measurement and Applied Research*, Washington, DC: American Psychological Association.

Crossen, C. (2006), "How Immigration Evolved as the Nation Grew and Changed," in *The Wall Street Journal*, 9 January 2006.

De Tocqueville, A. (1835, copyright 1945), *Democracy in America,* [Henry Reeve Text as revised by Frances Bowen and Phillips Bradley], New York: Alfred A. Knopf.

Eade, J. (Ed) (1997), *Living in the Global City: globalization as a local process,* London: Routledge.

Falicov, C. J. (1988), *Family Transitions: continuity and change over the life course,* New York: Guilford Press.

Fox, S. and Livingston, G. (2007), *Latinos Online,* Washington, DC: Pew Hispanic Center.

Fram, A. (2007), "Some US Muslims Say Suicide Attacks OK," in *AOL News*, via Washington, DC: Associated Press.

Friedman, T. L. (2006), *The World is Flat: a brief history of the twenty-first century,* New York: Farrar, Straus and Giroux.

Garcia Canclini, N. (1995), *Hybrid Cultures: strategies for entering and leaving modernity,* Minneapolis, MN: University of Minnesota Press.

Geliner, E. (1981), *The Muslim Society,* New York: Cambridge University Press.

Gergen, K. J. (1991), *The Saturated Self: dilemmas of identity in contemporary life,* New York: Basic Books.

Giddens, A. (1991), *Modernity and Self-Identity: self and society in the late modern age,* Cambridge: Polity Press.

Gordon, M. M. (1964), *Assimilation in American Life: the role of race, religion and national origins,* New York: Oxford University Press.

Graves, T. (1967), "Psychological acculturation in a tri-ethnic community." *South-western Journal of Anthropology* 23, pp. 337-350.

Haddad, Y. Y. and Lummis, A. T. (1987), *Islamic Values in the United States: a comparative study,* New York: Oxford University Press.

Hall, S. (1993), "Culture, Community, Nation," in *Cultural Studies* 7, no. 3, pp. 349-363.

Hallowell, A. I. (1945), "Sociopsychological aspects of acculturation." In R. Linton (Ed.) *The science of man in the world crisis* (pp. 310-332), New York: Columbia University Press.

Hannerz, U. (1990), "Cosmopolitans and Locals in World Culture," in Featherstone (Ed.), *Global Culture*, London: Routledge.

Hassan, A. G. (2000), *American Muslims: the new generation,* New York: Continuum.

House, K. E. (2007), "For Saudi Women, A Whiff of Change," in *The Wall Street Journal*, 7 April 2007, New York: Dow Jones and Company.

Hsu, F. L. K. (1955), *Americans and Chinese,* London: Cresset Press.

International Organization for Migration (2005), *Regional and Country Figures,* on website: http://www.iom.int/jahia/page255.html.

Islamic Council of North America (2006), *Islam Explained,* ICNA brochure, Piscataway, NJ.

Kahn, J. S. (1995), *Culture, Multiculture, Postculture,* Thousand Oaks, CA: Sage.

Kim, B. S. and Abreu, J. M. (2001), "Acculturation Measurement: Theory, Current Instruments and Future Directions," in J. G. Ponterotto, J. M. Casas, L. A. Suzuki and C. Alexander (Eds), *Handbook of Multicultural Counseling*, 2nd Edition, Thousand Oaks, CA: Sage.

Kim, U. & Berry, J. W. (1986), "Predictors of acculturative stress among Korean immigrants in Toronto," in L. Ekstrand (Ed.), *Ethnic minorities and immigrants*, (pp. 159-170), Lisse, The Netherlands: Swets & Zeitlinger.

Korzenny, F. and Korzenny, B. A. (2004), *Hispanic Marketing: A Cultural Perspective*, Oxford, England: Elsevier.

Kronemer, A. and Wolfe, M. (2002), *Muhammad: legacy of a Prophet*, Washington, DC: Public Broadcasting System (DVD of a documentary program originally prepared for television).

Kronholz, J. (2006), "Hispanics Gain in Census," *The Wall Street Journal*, 10 May 2006.

Leonard, K. I. (2003), *Muslims in the United States: the state of research*, New York: Russell Sage Foundation.

Lewellen, T. C. (2002), *The Anthropology of Globalization*, Westport: Bergin & Garvey.

Lombardi, C. (2007), *Mobile Browsing Becoming Mainstream*, from website: http://news.com.com/2102-1039_3-6062365.html?tag= st.util.print

Marin, G. and Gamba, R. J. (2003), "Acculturation and Changes in Cultural Values," in K. M. Chun, P. Balls Organista and G. Marin (Eds), *Acculturation: Advances in Theory, Measurement and Applied Research*, Washington, DC: American Psychological Association.

Morley, D. and Robins, K. (1995), *Spaces of Identity: global media, electronic landscapes and cultural boundaries*, London: Routledge.

Navia, P. and Zweifel, T. D. (2004), *I Want My MTV: freedom of information and democracy*, taken from website: http://www.google.com/ search?Q=international+television+set+penetration&hl=en&ie=u

Netcraft Web Server Survey Archives (2007), *May 2007 Web Server Survey*, from webite: http://news.netcraft.com/archives/web_server_ survey.html

Padilla, A. (1980), *Acculturation: Theory, models and some new findings*. Boulder, CO: Westview.

Passel, J. S. (2006), *The Size and Characteristics of the Unauthorized Migrant Population in the U.S.*, Research Report, Washington, DC: Pew Hispanic Center.

Passel, J. S. and Suro, R. (2005), *Rise, Peak and Decline: Trends in U. S. Immigration, 1992-2004*, Washington, DC: Pew Hispanic Center.

Pew Hispanic Center (2005), *Hispanic Trends: A People in Motion*, website: http://pewhispanic.org/reports/report.php?ReportID=40.

Pew (2007), *Muslim Americans: middle class and mostly mainstream,* Washington, DC: Pew Research Center.

Pew (2007A), *Public Espresses Mixed Views of Islam, Mormonism,* Washington, DC: Pew Research Center.

Phinney, J. S. (2003), *Ethnic Identity and Acculturation,* in K. M. Chun, P. Balls Organista and G. Marin (Eds), *Acculturation: Advances in Theory, Measurement and Applied Research,* Washington, DC: American Psychological Association.

Public Broadcasting System (2002), *Muhammad: legacy of a Prophet* (DVD of a television program), Washington, DC: PBS.

Ramirez, R. R. (2004), *We the People: Hispanics in the United States,* Washington, DC: US Bureau of the Census.

Ramos, J. (2000), *The Other Face of America,* New York: Rayo, an imprint of Harper-Collins.

Redfield, R., Linton, R., and Herskovits, M. (1936), Memorandum for the study of acculturation. *American Anthropologist* 38, 149-152.

Reeves, T. J. & Bennett, C. E. (2004), *We the People: Asians in the United States,* Washington, DC: US Bureau of the Census.

Richman, J., Gaviria, M., Flaherty, J., Birz, S., and Wintrob, R. (1987), "The process of acculturation: Theoretical perspectives and an empirical investigation in Peru," *Social Science Medicine* 25, 839-847.

Rushdie, S. (1991), *Imaginary Homelands,* London: Penguin.

Ryder, A., Alden, L., and Paulhus, D. (2000), "Is acculturation unidimensional or bi-dimensional?: a head-to-head comparison in the prediction of personality, self-identity and adjustment," *Journal of Personality and Social Psychology* 79, 49-65.

Sabogal, F., Marin, G., Otero-Sabogal, R., VanOss Marin, B., and Perez-Stable, E.J. (1987), "Hispanic Familialism and acculturation: what changes and what doesn't?" in *Hispanic Journal of Behavioural Sciences* 9, pp. 397-412.

Sanchez, J. and Fernandez, D. (1993), "Acculturative Stress Among Hispanics: A bi-dimensional model of ethnic identification," *Journal of Applied Social Psychology* 23, 660-670.

Santisteban, D. A. and Mitrani, V. B. (2003), *The Influence of Acculturation Processes on the Family,* in K. M. Chun, P. Balls Organista and G. Marin (Eds), *Acculturation: Advances in Theory, Measurement and Applied Research,* Washington, DC: American Psychological Association.

Sharma, A. (2007), "What's New in Wireless: a look at mobile devices and services you can expect in the next year—and beyond," in *The Wall Street Journal*, 26 March 2007, Technology Supplement, New York: Dow Jones and Company.

Shohat, E. (2006), *Taboo Memories, Diasporic Voices*, Durham, NC: Duke University Press.

Social Science Research Council (1954), "Acculturation: an exploratory formulation," *American Anthropologist* 56, 973-1002.

Sommerlad, E. and Berry, J. W. (1970), "The role of ethnic identification in distinguishing between attitudes towards assimilation and integration." *Human Relations* 23.

Sosa, L. (1999), *The Americano Dream*, New York: Plume, an imprint of Penguin Books.

Spindler, L. and Spindler, G. (1967), "Male and female adaptations in culture change: Menomini," In R. Hunt (Ed.) *Personalities and cultures*, New York: Natural History Press.

Suarez-Orozco, M. (2001), "Everything You Ever Wanted to Know About Assimilation but Were Afraid to Ask," quoted in Trimble, J. E., *Introduction: Social Change and Acculturation,* in K. M. Chun, P. Balls Organista and G. Marin (Eds), *Acculturation: Advances in Theory, Measurement and Applied Research*, Washington, DC: American Psychological Association.

Sue, S. (2003), *Foreword,* in K. M. Chun, P. Balls Organista and G. Marin (Eds), *Acculturation: Advances in Theory, Measurement and Applied Research*, Washington, DC: American Psychological Association.

Teske, R. and Nelson, B. (1974), "Acculturation and assimilation: a clarification," *American Ethnologist* 1, 351-368.

Thernstrom, S. (2004), "Rediscovering the Melting Pot—still going strong," in Jacoby, T. (Ed.) (2004), *Reinventing the Melting Pot*, New York: Basic Books.

Tomlinson, J. (1999), *Globalization and Culture,* Chicago: University of Chicago Press.

Trimble, J. E. (2003), "Introduction: Social Change and Acculturation," in K. M. Chun, P. Balls Organista and G. Marin (Eds), *Acculturation: Advances in Theory, Measurement and Applied Research*, Washington, DC: American Psychological Association.

United Nations (2006), *World Migrant Stock: The 2005 Revision Population Database,* in website: http://esa.un.org/migration/p2k0data.asp

US Bureau of the Census (1999), Data for 1960 come from *Region of the Foreign-Born Population: 1850 to 1930 and 1960 to 1990*, Table 2. Washington, DC.

US Bureau of the Census (2000), Data for 2000 are calculated to match, from *Data Set: Census 2000*, Summary File 4, QT-P14. Nativity, Citizenship, Year of Entry, and Region of Birth: 2000. Washington, DC.

US Bureau of the Census (2004 A), *American FactFinder, PEOPLE: Race and Ethnicity*. Contained in website: http://factfinder.census. gov/jsp/saff/SAFFInfo.jsp?_pageId=tp9_ race_ethnicity, Washington, DC.

US Bureau of the Census (2004 B), table 1, *US Interim Projections by Age, Sex, Race and Hispanic Origin,* Washington, DC.

US Bureau of the Census (2006), web site home page: www.census.gov.

Valdes, Isabel (1991), Presentation by Hispanic Market Connections, Los Altos, CA, based on earlier work by Bronfenbrenner, U. (1979), *Ecology of Human Development: experiments by nature and design,* Cambridge, MA: Harvard University Press and Falicov, C. J. (1988), *Family Transitions: continuity and change over the life course,* New York: Guilford Press.

Williams, C. and Berry, J. (1991), "Primary Prevention of Accurative Stress Among Refugees," *American Psychologist* 46, pp. 632-641, quoted in Berry (2003), p. 30.

Wormser, R. (1994), *American Islam: growing up Muslim in America,* New York: Walker and Company.

Zane, N. and Mak, W. (2003), "Major Approaches to the Measurement of Acculturation Among Ethnic Minority Populations: A content analysis and an alternative Empirical strategy," in K. M. Chun, P. Balls Organista and G. Marin (Eds), *Acculturation: Advances in Theory, Measurement and Applied Research*, Washington, DC: American Psychological Association.

Zangwill, I. (1925), *The Melting Pot: a drama in four acts,* New York, AMS Press.

Zogby, J., Bruce, J., Wittman, R., and Peck, W. W. (2004), *Muslims in the American Public Square: shifting political winds and fallout from 9/11, Afghanistan and Iraq,* Washington, DC: Center for Muslim-Christian Understanding, Georgetown University.

Index

About the Author

Marvin Shaub earned a BA from Cornell University in 1962 and an MBA from The Harvard Business School in 1964. He then pursued a successful business career spanning over 40 years working in The United States, Europe and Japan in the roles of corporate executive, entrepreneur, consultant and speaker. At age 65, in lieu of retirement, he pursued and was awarded a Ph.D.—Doctor of Social Sciences—from Tilburg University in The Netherlands. Currently he teaches international business at Montclair State University in New Jersey. An American citizen, he lives with his wife, a naturalized Japanese-American, and a teenage daughter (one of four children) in Princeton, NJ, USA.